PRAISE FO
ENTHUSIASM UN

"Enthusiasm Unchained was a brilliant read. As a young black professional, this book provided active examples on how to overcome fallacious stereotypes formed in and outside the corporate realm. Enthusiasm Unchained provide the tools black professionals need to embrace and rise above the daily challenges faced in the corporate world. More distinctively, the book highlights the need to maintain your identity and to always deliver high performance. This is a must read book and I will definitely be using tips learned from the book from today onwards"!

Ainsley Bell
CEO, Mania Movements

If you are a black professional seeking to climb the corporate ladder, "Enthusiasm Unchained" is the ideal book for you. It is packed with tips and practical tools to unleash your full potential as you navigate pitfalls, office politics and challenges. The author's approach and use of examples is refreshing and inspiring.

Duane Wright
Relationship Manager, Commercial Banking

"Romeo Effs unravels the mysteries of career success for black professionals, and reveals that luck and magic are not the ingredients for success, but instead sets out a methodical process that can be learned and replicated. Whether you have been employed for a long time and you're feeling stagnant in your career or you are a graduate just entering the corporate world, there are very important lessons and tools contained in this book that can make your quest towards career success far easier".

Rashada Harry
Vodafone Global Enterprise
Director, Your Future, Your Ambition

"Enthusiasm Unchained has tapped in to the heart of the issue being faced by black professionals in the corporate world and has distilled it in a way that is easy to understand. The tools and processes in the book are simple yet effective and will make a massive change in the life of those who implement them. I certainly will be implementing them in my professional and personal life".

Alterrell Mills
Harvard MBA Student and Former Walls Street Professional

"Not only will this book help young black professional it will help young blacks that have lost their way in life. This book is helpful, instructive and encourages black people to understand who they are and where their from. I enjoyed reading it and I sincerely hope others will feel as I did. Well done love and thank you for doing your bit to encourage young black professionals whatever background they come from".

Diana Antwi
Credit Control, Belfour Beatty

"This book (Enthusiasm Unchained) should be a mandatory read for all black professionals. It shows how to cut through the fog of uncertainty and lack of knowledge on career success that surrounds a lot of black professionals in the corporate world. Romeo outlines a rigorous approach with practical prescriptions that are easy to understand and if used could make the journey up the corporate ladder less burdensome for black professionals. This book could do more to boast black professionals personal and career aspirations than any other book written in years".

O'Brien Dennis
Executive Director – Obrien Dennis Foundation
Author, Understanding Male Sexual Abuse

What I like about Enthusiasm Unchained is that, Romeo is a straight talker and tells it as it is. The book shows how to break the mold of the corporate world; unshackling negative thoughts that can hold you back so you have the time to dream and think bigger. The book gives real advice and implementable tools on how to be positive and deliver high performance in all situations, and be the best you can be. An excellent read!

Wincie Knight
Social Responsibility Manager, Nichelodeon

ENTHUSIASM UNCHAINED

UNSHACKLING PERSONAL AND PROFESSIONAL SUCCESS A BLACK PERSPECTIVE

ROMEO EFFS

ST. PAUL PUBLISHING

First published in 2014 by: RSPE Ltd. t/a St. Paul Publishing,
Alberminster House, 38-40 Syndenham Road, Croydon, Greater London, CR0 2EF
Email (for orders and customers service enquires): *booksales@rspegroup.com*

A catalogue record for this book is available from the
British Library and the Library of Congress.

978-0-9932928-0-4 Paperback

978-0-9932928-1-1 eBook-Mobi

978-0-9932928-2-8 eBook-ePub

978-0-9932928-3-5 eBook-eReader

978-0-9932928-4-2 eBook-PDF

Typeset by *wordzworth.com*
Printed and bound by Ingram Spark

Dedication

For my Grandmother – Iris May Bruff, my soul mate, my rock and my sand, my friend and confidante, my spiritual guide, my teacher, my motivator, and my inspirer, who taught me that through faith, anything is possible, and that I can become anybody and do anything, and without whom I would not be what I am today. Love you always Granny.

For my dear sweet Mom – Inet Jane Effs, my professor, my provider, my defender, my rock, and the one who always believed in me and never gave up on me, (even when my grades were not that great and I would disobey her), my best friend, my Michelin star chef, my healer and my carer. You sacrificed and gave up so much for me, so I could have the best education, the best life, and become the man I am today. My love for you is like an eternal flame that can never die.

CONTENTS

A Must Read
Introduction

"They themselves are makers of themselves" by virtue of the thoughts which they choose and encourage; that mind is the master weaver, both of the inner garment of character and the outer garment of circumstance, and that, as they may have hitherto woven in ignorance and pain they may now weave in enlightenment and happiness.

James Allen – As a Man Thinketh

I am compelled start out by saying that this book is not a panacea, but is a practical toolbox of techniques to help you. I am sharing insight garnered from my over 25 plus years of experience as a senior executive, serial entrepreneur, coach, mentor, inspirational speaker and life ups and downs. The book is geared at inspiring you to reshape your mind-set and remove blockages; negative labels and self-affirmed stereotypes that hold you back from achieving phenomenal personal and professional success.

In this book you will learn how to:

- Dream bigger and dig deeper.
- Develop the right mind-set for career progression and success.
- Deal with stereotypical issues faced by many black professionals in the workplace.
- Roadmap your vision and set I.D.E.A.L. goals
- Use the right tools to plan your dream career path.
- Take decisive action now to become a high performer.
- Use powerful tools to make quantum leaps in your personal life.
- Deliver value, phenomenal results and leave memorable experiences.
- Leave people wanting more of you wherever you go.

Throughout life we will meet people who keep telling us what we can or cannot become. Sometimes this is good, but more often than not, we are labelled negatively. Yet, it is only when we affirm these negative labels that they seep into our subconscious and paralyse our progress. We cannot stop these daggers from being thrown, but we can choose to armour ourselves with the right tools, techniques, positive thoughts, images and self-confidence.

The only power that negative labels have over you is the power you give them. Stop talking to people about them. Stop repeating them. Only then you will remove them. Words are like seeds; if you dwell on them long enough, they take root and become what was said, good or bad.

The only purpose that negative labels have in our lives is to serve as positive motivators. Use those negative labels to seek what I call "positive revenge" to prove naysayers wrong. Let them realise that no matter what negative labels they paste on you it will not hinder you from realising your greatness and #CreatingAmazing.

As a teenager, Walt Disney's Art teacher told him that he lacked imagination and creativity. Yet he removed that label and *created* the iconic Walt Disney brand we know today.

Oprah Winfrey was told that she could not become a television presenter, yet became one of history's most successful and wealthiest media moguls.

Winston Churchill failed the 6th grade and was told he was not smart enough. He went on to become one of the greatest leaders that we have ever seen.

What is the common denominator between these people? They chose to remove all the negative labels that others sought to affix to them. They chose to use those negative labels as motivators to prove the naysayers wrong and achieve greatness in their own right. Don't allow anyone to stereotype you or putt you in a box.

All of us have an inner force that pushes us towards what we are on this earth to do. Each of us has a unique and different purpose on this earth. That is why no two of us are created identical. Our exact genetically make up, have never been made before and will never be repeated. We are all unique and different in our own ways. It's this uniqueness and difference that makes us who we are, and it's this inner force we are all born with that helps to bring out that uniqueness and difference.

Think back to when you were a child, you thought that anything was possible; there were no limits, no boundaries. I thought I would fly to the moon and that I was superman fighting off evil. I even thought that I was the world's best dancer and experimented with this at school for a while and was good at it. We all made up different stories from our thoughts, and the stories of our friends and siblings were all different.

As we grew up and got influenced by our environment and develop anxieties, this force that use to propel us to think without limits, wore off and got trapped. We no longer make it drive our thought pattern and hence we feel lost and incomplete. This lack of clarity of who we are and what makes us unique and different is the reason most persons are so unhappy in their careers, in the business they operate and in their life generally. They trap this inner force, controlling it because of what society dictates, because of family pressure or peer pressure and negative labels. I did that for a number of years until I rekindled that inner force and ultimately freed it to shine bright and illuminate the world with what I am doing now – educating, training and inspiring others.

In order for you to create amazing and find true success, you need to learn who you really are and reconnect with that inner force. You have to know who you are and what your purpose on this earth is with clarity, in order for you to find your way to the proper career path and be good at it, choose and operate the right business successfully and make others around you happy. Society and our environment so easily influence us, so the skills required to create this future must be continuously learnt, nurtured and be cultivated. You get the mind, quality of brain and successes you deserve in life through your action or in action. Don't be fooled, genetics, education and brilliance alone will never be the force that determines your greatness or your success.

Recent research in neuroscience has shown that the brain is not hard wired as we were meant to believe, but is "plastic". What this means is that our thoughts determines our "mental landscape". This mental landscape or mind-set that is formed by our thoughts can determine our health, wealth, prosperity and ultimately what we determine as success.

This proves that we are ultimately responsible for everything that happens to us in life. We can and need to create our own success world whether as professionals in a corporate setting or as an entrepreneur. Our thoughts are the most powerful force in the universe. So with our thoughts we can create amazing by unshackling that masterful mind within, through the actions we take.

Once you have learnt and cultivated how to do that it will help you to find your way to your inclination, your purpose, and you will be taking that first step towards creating an amazing life.

If you remain stagnant, do nothing, don't learn and cultivate this mental landscape, you will conform to social norms and stereotypes, and listen to the pressures all around you, and end up choosing a career path, partner or business idea because of peer pressure and what society thinks of you or think is best for you. If this happens you will end being frustrated and miserable and internally dead.

What you need to understand however is that the process of creating amazing is not linear. Everything that happens to you in your lives, good or bad happens for a reason and is serving a purpose. You should see these circumstances as forms of instructions, taking you towards your inclination. These circumstances in life happen to bringing forth your difference and uniqueness, and to help you to nurture and grow that seed that has been planted in your heart, that purpose why we were created.

As long as you are alive you are in constant change. So the process of #CreateAmazing is evolutionary. The more we grow the more we will need to learn and grow, because changes and circumstance will force us to adapt. The moment we rest on our laurels, thinking we have arrived, apart of our mind starts to decay and die.

Don't talk about where you are from, your colour, what people say or think about you, that's a fallacy. There are many persons who were told that they would not achieve anything who are very successful in their own right, created amazing and left a lasting impression on this planet. Look at some of these incredible examples I mentioned earlier. The only way to find real and lasting success is to rekindle that inner force, nurture it by continually developing and learning, and cultivate it by changing and adapting. All those above did just this.

You should live your live with one simple mantra.

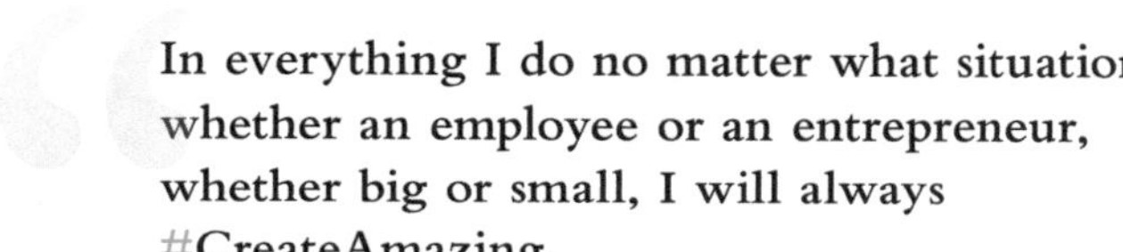

> **In everything I do no matter what situation whether an employee or an entrepreneur, whether big or small, I will always #CreateAmazing.**

Why – Because that is what we are created to do. To #CreateAmazing greatness, #CreateAmazing memories and #CreateAmazing lasting legacy. Each of us holds our future in our own hands; we are all born with the capability to create our own amazing successful world.

When you #CreateAmazing you leave positive and lasting memorable experiences.

When you #CreateAmazing the impact and footprint you leave in the world cannot be easily erased.

When you #CreateAmazing you push the boundaries and deliver the epitome of quality, high performance and brilliance.

You must be relentless in your desire to push boundaries, go further and constantly strive to #CreateAmazing daily.

It is never too late to start this process!
Are you ready for lasting transformation?
Dig deep and enjoy the book!

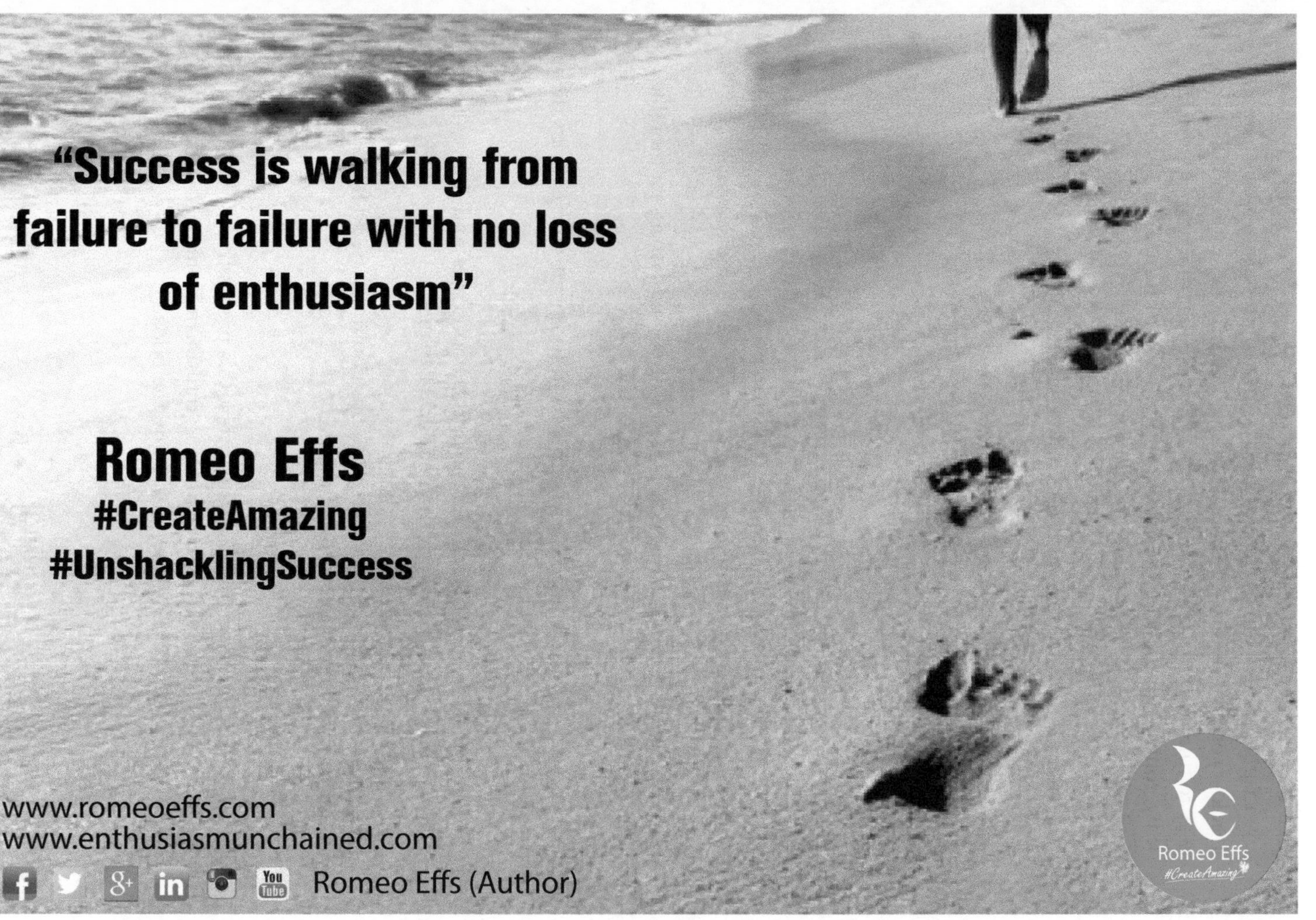
"Success is walking from
failure to failure with no loss
of enthusiasm"
Romeo Effs
#CreateAmazing
#UnshacklingSuccess
www.romeoeffs.com
www.enthusiasmunchained.com
Romeo Effs (Author)
Romeo Effs
#CreateAmazing

ONE

Accept That You Are Different

Accept that you're different. You are a go-getter, an achiever, a risk taker, and a performer – A Bright Spark who was born to stand out. Embrace and run with your uniqueness. No one should be able to tell you who you are or who you can become. They may advise and counsel, but not instruct you on what you can or cannot achieve. Who or what you become is solely up to you.

Romeo Effs

Determination is undoubtedly one of the overarching traits of the black race, and so are Bright Sparks. Bright sparks are people, just like you, who are witty, intelligent, dreamers, ambitious, driven and with loads of common sense. They are full of tenacity and courage to have a vision for themselves and the world, and move towards it with zest, purpose and determination.

I first heard the term "bright spark" in primary school when teachers referred to outstanding pupils as "bright sparks". Thinking of the word, I would envision illuminating objects such as diamonds, the sun, or the reflection of the moonlight on the ocean; the stars – things that shine bright and change the nature of the world. Just like you.

Being a bright spark is not easy. You may be ridiculed, teased and bullied. You are often misjudged as a know-it-all, overconfident or arrogant. As a bright spark, you need to learn how to strike a balance between your beliefs, and the principles of life; keep your morals and ethics intact so that the constant scrutiny of naysayers will not disillusion you.

Ambitious people of colour (referred to as 'black bright sparks' throughout this book) can be very difficult to contextualise, especially in a country or society that sees a driven black person as angry and with a chip on their shoulder. Not to mention the stock of stereotypical behaviours that is dumped on their heads. These notions tend to diminish the spark and cause you to settle for less than you deserve, what you desire or what you can become. Just know and believe that you are a "black bright spark".

A "black bright spark", of any tribe or background is born to stand out. You are born to be great, and to make a significant difference in this world. You are born to be on fire, so set this world ablaze with your difference, your uniqueness, your panache and your performance. Let no one tell you as a "black bright spark", who you can become, or what you can accomplish. You are the master of your destiny, the Michelangelo of your life; the ceiling of the Sistine Chapel you are painting is your life.

We are from a long line of empire builders

Black people come from a long line of great achievers and empire builders. Throughout history, we have always been viewed, whether positively or negatively, as different – oddities. The world is full of people with differences of opinions, beliefs, attitudes, and ways of doing things. As a "black bright spark", you should use this uniqueness to your advantage to achieve your goals, aspirations, and dreams. One of the greatest things I learnt from my grandmother (whom you will see I refer to a lot throughout this book) is that "in every adversity there is opportunity". Take the negatives that people project about you and make them work to your advantage. When you are told you cannot do something or cannot become the person you want to become, go all out to prove that person wrong.

Flip the Script

I recall a story a "black bright spark" once told me that while attending school the teacher asked him what he wanted to become. He said he wanted to become a lawyer, and the teacher's advice was that people from his background could not become Lawyers. He was advised to set his ambitions to become a bus conductor or porter. Today, this "black bright spark" is a Barrister. Good on him, and well done for flipping the script and proving this teacher wrong.

There are numerous inventors and achievers from every walk of life to whom we can look for inspiration. Fashion your dreams off daring empire builders, world champions, conquerors, and billionaires, world leaders who had a dream and saw it through, against all the odds.

They have all faced failures and difficulties and have had to deal with some sort of prejudice or the other on their success journey. Every experience, good or bad, is a valuable lesson that makes you stronger and more resilient, and also serves to push you towards your higher purpose.

Our legacy as a black race is rich, vibrant and explosive. It runs so deep that we cannot help but want to explode into success. History teaches us that as a people we have always gone through turmoil, divisions, separation, humiliation, suffering and trials. Through all this, we had the determination and the innate belief that we were great and would be better.

As they say in Jamaica, "betta mus come" (better times will come). We persevered, struggled and survived against all odds and are now unstoppable masters of our destiny.

Who falls in the category of a "black bright spark"?

I have experienced the difficulties you have had in making these dreams come true, especially in corporate life. I have lived some of these unfortunate circumstances, but I have never allowed them to deter me from pushing forward with power of purpose and determination. You should do the same. There are millions, if not billions, of "black bright sparks throughout the world. They are educated, intelligent, high-performers who want to and intend to achieve phenomenal success and leave a lasting legacy. "Black bright sparks" strive for greatness in whatever they do and continuously move the goalpost each time they score a personal victory. They can be found in all aspects of society, whether they accept that they are a "bright spark" or not. Take a look around your office or your industry, and I am sure you will be able to find at least one.

The road to success is littered with many "black bright sparks"

As a "black bright spark", you are not alone, and you can learn how to manage your zest for success with the right tools and process. This book is not a "Fix it all", but it will show you a few good tricks and tools that you can use on your success journey, working smarter not harder. Many others and I have used these tools and strategies, and they have helped on the journey to hitting those milestones and achieving those goals. These tools will help you reach for and get closer to your vision, that dangling carrot (I will expand more on this in Chapter 6), you see as success.

Take a look at some "black bright sparks" that are making waves in the world today at our "Black Bright Spark" page on Facebook. See that you are not alone. Others have achieved greatness before you. They are of different ages and from different countries, but their journeys and stories are similar.

In school, I was told I was a bright spark, not necessarily always at the top of the class, but always never too far from the top. I always had huge ambitions and aimed high. I was bullied because I was overweight. I was never selected for any team during PE (physical education) or for any of the school sports teams. This happened all the way through my Primary & High school years. But I used that to my advantage and focused on academics. I wanted to prove the doubters wrong and show them that I could be good at something. I read widely and practised math constantly, though I am still not very good at it today ☺. I did my homework every night and was always the first to volunteer in class to answer a problem. I learned at an early age that participating helped me to learn more because I could approach improvement based on feedback from the teacher.

I did not consider myself an overachiever or a bright spark until one of my best friends Phil chose those words to describe me many years ago. It then dawned on me that I was indeed a bit of an overachiever and indeed a "Black Bright Spark". You see an overachiever is someone who is constantly redrawing and exceeding the boundaries of their own possibilities.

Looking back over my short life, I have achieved some phenomenal feats, and I can praise myself as having done well. I have hit 90% of all the milestones that I have set in my career, business, social, and political life. I have redrawn the boundaries, most times more complex, to add momentum and challenge to my success journey.

I have encountered, worked with, developed and learnt from many "black bright sparks", and they have propelled me along the way. At 19 years old, upon completing my A-Levels, I began working in the airline industry.

I aspired and set an objective to become a Lead Agent (Supervisor) after one year. I asked my fellow colleagues, most of who had been in the industry for a long time, what was required to get to this goal. I mapped out what it took, the timeframe, and all the courses that I would need to take in order to make this happen, and it did. I had no idea of all the current philosophies, processes, techniques, tools and terminologies that I now use with the people I mentor, coach and develop. All I knew then was that I wanted to achieve something greater than where I was. I wanted bigger responsibilities, the authority, and the organisational status that came with it.

This, however, was just a stepping-stone to my much bigger goal of being a Senior Manager by the age of 25. I also blew that goal out of the water, and I was an Executive in the airline industry by that age. At the same time, I was involved in politics, as an advisor, researcher, and speechwriter for Members of Parliament and Senators. I was General Secretary of a major political think-tank travelling the world to meet with world leaders and other young political leaders. I had also started one of the most successful event management companies, doing music festivals with global music icons, and producing movies with Hollywood stars, and besides these, there are many other success stories. So, I guess looking back on all that I have done and accomplished, I can be proud to accept that I am indeed an overachiever and a "black bright spark".

Learn to accept yourself, you "black bright spark!"

Accepting you for who you are, and knowing you can achieve anything and become whoever you want to become, is the first step on this success journey as a "black bright spark". You will have different circumstances, hopes, dreams and visions than those of your friends and peers. You may be from a much poorer background, attended different schools, lived in different communities, have different types of parents, and differ in religious beliefs and social values, but the one thing that binds you all is that drive, belief, and "power of purpose and determination" to succeed.

It is part of who you are; it is part of your DNA as a descendent of the black race. This hunger to explode into success, to be great, and achieve phenomenal things is not a mistake. It is what you were born to do: achieve phenomenal success, and change the landscape of this universe for the better. You have to believe and accept that whole-heartedly. You are different, and people will see you as that – different, weird, sometimes arrogant, sometimes overzealous, sometimes too calm, full of direction and drive, sometimes fun, and sometimes boring. Don't fight it. Embrace it and move on.

Learn to accept that your ambitions and dreams will or might be bigger and more far-reaching than those around you. That is just how it is. Just because your dreams and passion for success are much bigger than your friends, family or colleagues dreams does not make yours better or make theirs less important. What is important is that they also have dreams, and they also have a vision of what success is for them. Don't diminish your dreams and ambitions to suit others or to seem part of the in crowd. Dreams and ambitions are powerful things, and when mixed with power of purpose and determination, and a burning desire, they can be translated into untold success and riches.

Napoleon Hill, in his book *Think and Grow Rich*, puts it perfectly – "whatever the mind of man can conceive and believe, it can achieve". I am a firm believer of this, and if you want to achieve what you conceive as success, you have to embed this within your thoughts.

Everything you want to be, you already are. All you are doing is discovering that journey to becoming a greater success. So shine your light, illuminate, and make the world bright with your exuberance … accept yourself for who you are and give birth to the genius in you. The night sky is not lit by one star, but by billions of bright stars, so there are billions of dreams, each with its own path to success.

The corporate world can be a very unfriendly place to "black bright sparks". Many times it's because we either underestimate the devious and calculated deception that can be dished out when people are threatened by us, or more importantly, we ourselves fail to understand that there is a game to be played to make it in the corporate rat race. Learning to accept yourself, knowing you are passionate and yearning for success are some of the first challenges you will have to overcome to dealing with the challenges you will face in the corporate world, in order to be a winner. Dealing with this successfully will lead to the delivery of phenomenal results, and you leaving memorable experiences and #CreateAmazing.

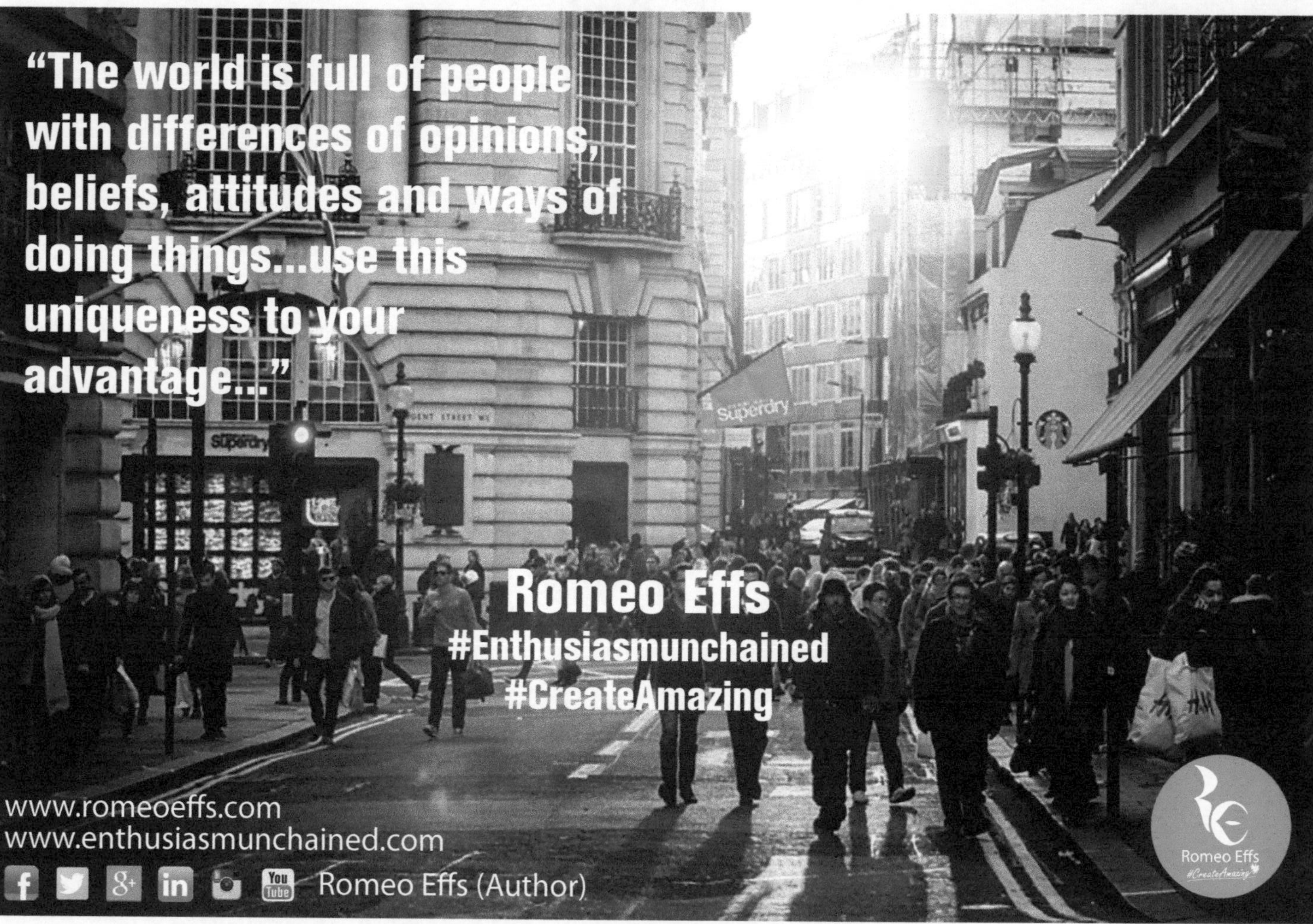
"The world is full of people
with differences of opinions,
beliefs, attitudes and ways of
doing things...use this
uniqueness to your
advantage..."
Romeo Effs
#Enthusiasmunchained
#CreateAmazing
www.romeoeffs.com
www.enthusiasmunchained.com
Romeo Effs (Author)
Romeo Effs
#CreateAmazing
Superdry

Please Listen & Watch
www.enthusiasmunchained.com/EU1

TWO

Norms: The Corporate vs. Social Dichotomy

"When in Rome do as the Romans do".

St. Ambrose 387 A.D.

What are Corporate Norms?

Norms can be defined as attitudes and behaviours common to members of a particular group. It is what that group believes is "normal".

For example, in Caribbean and African customs, there are norms about how we speak and deal with our elders. We would refer to them as "Uncle" or "Auntie" even if we don't know them, but the custom sees that as "normal" behaviour towards them. Your choice of words, your tone, and your body language are all norm-based, and will be different when you speak to your children, your partner, your boss, or work colleague.

Nearly everything in human society is governed by norms of some kind. These norms differ from group to group. Norms vary so much that how we conduct ourselves in the community we live is not necessarily the same as how we conduct ourselves in another community we may visit. This is why it feels so strange to go to a very different culture, where their norms are so different to what we are used to – but it is normal to them.

As a group, the corporate world has its own set of norms that govern how it operates, breathes, thrives and survives. Even in some large corporates, the various departments or divisions have differing norms, but there are some general corporate norms that permeate all corporates, and if not followed or adopted, will lead to frustration, and could even result in failure. As a "black bright spark", part of what you need to learn and understand is not just the task of the job you must perform, but also the unwritten rules – the norms – associated with that task, the organisation, team or group you are part of.

Norms in any group are important as it helps to keep order, discipline, and get everyone fixated on the process of operating and moving towards achieving an objective. That objective could be profit, reputation or something more elusive such as eternal life.

Organisations rely heavily on their norms to survive. They refer to it as the "culture" of the organisation. During the interview stages for a job, a large part of the process, unknown to many, is to see whether or not you will be a "good cultural fit". Being a "good cultural fit" is key to an organisation, as it prevents turmoil within the organisation. Someone that does not conform to the organisation's culture results in team disruptions and valuable time wasted trying to correct or get team dynamics right. From experience, this is not a good place to be when you are managing a team or as a member of a team. As a "black bright spark", understanding the difference between your social norms and corporate norms is vital if you are to succeed and win in the corporate rat race.

There are certain activities that I would not consider "corporate culture/ norms", and in any shape, form or fashion, and would not tolerate these behaviours within any organisation, neither as an employee, manager, or executive. These include activities such as bullying, unethical behaviour, discrimination of any kind, immoral behaviour, or undermining, though this is subjective. They do exist, and sometimes are overlooked or ignored, depending on who carries them out; but there are laws and HR policies that reinforce the dictum that these are non-conforming group norms and should not be practised.

The social/corporate norm dichotomy

Most of us Black Bright Sparks do not have parents who are corporate executives, although that is changing; so, these corporate behaviours and norms did not rub off on us naturally. Most of us would also have been brought up in communities with little or no exposure to corporate executives, and would know of only a few that we would see on TV or in the papers. So, our exposure to the way of the corporate world would have been limited prior to us getting there. That puts "black bright sparks" at a disadvantage.

As stated before, norms are the behaviour of a particular group. Therefore, our behaviours in the communities in which we live, our peers, and those with whom we associate dictate our norms. These behaviours, sometimes, conflict severely with the behaviours expected from us within the corporate world. This conflict can hinder your growth and progression within an organisation. This, in turn, can lead to frustration, and what I term, as "wild out" or "burn out" behaviour.

I was mentoring a "black bright spark" in a large FTSE company in which I worked. He was employed as a bid writer. He had been in the organisation for a few years and was very concerned as to why he had not yet been promoted even though each bid he wrote or contributed to would win a contract. Let me paint a picture: He had cornrows that he did about once per month, if that often. He had facial hair that was untidy. His shirt was always soiled and looked crushed as if he had slept in it the night before. He wore the same black suit to work for days, and the trousers had rips below the pockets at the front and the back. His tie was tied but hung loosely around his neck and the top button on his shirt was open. His fingernails were over-grown and dirty. I spoke to him several times about his attire, but he saw nothing wrong with it because he was just "expressing himself". His frustration came to a halt when the team expanded, and they hired two bid managers externally that he had to report to. These bid managers were not necessarily more intelligent or knew the job better than he. As a matter of fact, they had less experience and did not write and deliver bids at the standard he did. In one of our sessions, he began lamenting his frustration about this, so I had a quick chat with the Bid Director on his behalf. The Bid Director's comments were simple: "Although he delivers excellent work and knows his job more than anyone else on the team, there is no way we could put him in front of clients". I agreed totally with the Bid Director, and I told my mentee this in confidence.

He allowed some of his social norms to dictate his behaviour in the work place, resulting in him being overlooked for promotion even though he delivered phenomenal results. As "black bright sparks", you need to know that, for you, in this corporate rat race, you are a package, and no one thing will work on its own.

Although it took my mentee some time to realise and confirm this. As a "black bright spark", he heeded my advice and came in the office one Monday morning looking totally transformed. His hair was well done, facial hair was neat and groomed, and clothes were crisp and clean. He was noticed, and everyone in the office complimented him on his new look. He did not get a promotion at the company, but after a few more rounds of our mentoring sessions, he went on four months later to get a senior Bid Manager's role in another organisation. I guess he made a good first impression, and they saw him as a perfect "cultural fit".

Understanding that there is a clear difference between your social behaviour, the way you behave, speak and dress with your friends in the community in which you live and those of the corporate world is yet another key step in knowing how to successfully navigate this corporate rat race.

You bring Diversity…Whoopee! So what?

Most "black bright sparks" that I speak to, coach or mentor tend to have this false notion that their social norm brings "diversity" to an organisation. What needs to be crystal clear and thoroughly understood is that this behaviour is only accepted as diverse if it does not conflict with the already established corporate behaviour or culture. Once it brings the corporate culture or way of doing things in disrepute, you will be dismissed… Full stop!

Yes, you bring diversity in how you behave and conduct yourself, but these should be the deep-rooted values and beliefs that our parents, elders and forefathers taught us, not those that can be considered negative or disruptive to the flow of a team or organisation. Some of these include our attitudes around them and our mannerisms in talking and dealing with team members.

Yes, you bring diversity of thought leadership, experience and expertise. Diversity in thought leadership is what you should be striving to bring to an organisation and team. Of course, your culture, your beliefs, values and upbringing shape this diversity of thought leadership. Thought leadership should be about the positives that one can take from these areas of our society and use to make a positive and lasting impact on the team and the organisation, leaving "memorable experiences".

As a Manager at one of the big five consulting firms, I was usually the only black person in the room or sitting around the table discussing a proposal or a client's issue. I was once assigned to a team looking at redesigning the operating model for one of the world's largest logistics and parcel delivery companies. During the process of designing the presentation, I recommended that we make it less "consultative" in its approach and more "operational", so we could speak directly to the client's issues and less about what we have done and can deliver as a firm. Having owned and operated a transport and logistics company and with years of experience in the airline industry at a Senior level as well as having been involved in designing one of the most complex cargo networks in the Caribbean, I brought diverse thought leadership, based on my experiences and qualifications to bear, whilst also making a paradigm shift in how things "normally" work. The team was receptive (thank God), and the new approach was very well received, resulting in us being rewarded a very well paid piece of consultation work.

Yes, you bring diversity in how the organisation looks, feels and is perceived. But, make no mistake, there are many of you around who can fill that slot, so don't see this as an advantage. What you need to know is that for some organisations this is just a tick box exercise, so they can look good to the client and wider community; but it is not a genuine endeavour.

So, you being in the team only because you look different is not an advantage, but a disadvantage. You will still need to prove your worth if you are to survive and be successful in the corporate rat race. Furthermore, if the only reason you are part of a team or organisation is just to make it look diverse whilst enabling them to tick the ethnicity and corporate social responsibility box, then get out, and find a place where your worth and value is more important than your skin colour.

Yes, you bring diversity of working and delivering phenomenal results within the confines of the organisation's norms, values and principles. As a "black bright spark", this is what you should be known for. As black people, we have different perspectives on issues, and because of our struggles and upbringing, we also tend to see challenges through a different set of lens, usually coming up with solutions that others cannot. It is this dynamism that we should bring as a "diverse" member of an organisation or team, along with our blackness and the cultural, social difference and positives that come with it.

I recall having a chat with one of my female mentees, a "black bright spark" who was part of a team managing a large contract in a large facilities management company. The company had just won the contract for a large financial institution to manage the facilities of all the branch network and satellite offices in the UK. They were in the process of designing an operating model and the procedures for the cleaning staff.

This young lady grew up with a mother who was a cleaner. She remembered listening every day to the complaints of her and her mom's friends who were also cleaners, about the good, the bad, the shortcomings and the successes that they had to work and put up with. She also recalled going in to help her mother on weekends, when she was a teenager, to clean some of the offices her Mom was tasked to clean. With this wealth of first-hand knowledge and experience, she became an extremely valuable member of the Transition team, and eventually, went on to become one of the Contract Managers on the contract. This is a true example of how diverse experiences in a team can deliver win-win results.

It's our diverse values, beliefs, attitudes and positive behaviour that we should bring to the corporate world and the teams we are a part of. It's these diverse traits you need to infuse and emit if you feel that the norms of an organisation need tweaking, or changing completely for the better.

Grooming and Attire

One of the biggest issues I have observed in the corporate world (especially in the UK) with black people is our grooming and attire. Let's call a spade a spade (and I don't mean this to be offensive as it is an old phrase with racial connotations)! For most black individuals, this issue needs to be addressed seriously. Some women tend to wear weaves or wigs. In most instances, they are unkempt and look like a cat that has just been electrocuted.

For the most part, however, women tend to be much better attired in the work place than men, even though a man's corporate dress is simple and straightforward. So, I am going to deal exclusively with the men here.

Men, if you wear corn rows or need to have long hair for religious reasons e.g. dreads etc., be prepared to budget the money to have it done at least bi-weekly so that it looks neat, groomed and well kept. I have seen many successful black males with these hairstyles, and they always look well groomed and neat. Keep your hair groomed and at a length that is manageable; and when combed, it will look presentable and groomed. This goes even if you are not planning to enter corporate life but looking to start your own business. You will find it goes a long way when speaking to customers, prospective investors, and suppliers.

When it comes to grooming, a "black bright spark" must always dress the part (role) or more importantly above the part (role) he currently holds. In the same way, if you want to be promoted, you need to act and deliver those phenomenal results above your current status in the organisation (I will deal with this in a later chapter of the book). Your attire says a lot about you. It is usually the first impression someone gets of you, as they can see you coming from a distance. This will often tell them the kind of person you will be in the organisation. I'm not saying you should be one of those "looking good, but going nowhere" individuals. Employers quickly find out and discount these types of persons. What I am saying is that looking good, being well groomed, and well-attired sends a signal of confidence, even when you feel like you are dying inside. It sends signals that you are ambitious with a power of purpose and determination. When you are on the train or the bus, and you see a well-dressed black male or female, I am sure you look twice and wonder to yourself: Where are they going or what job do they do? They command your attention and your respect, even just for that brief moment that you are locked in the compartment of the train or the bus.

It's the same way in the corporate world; as a "black bright spark", you stand out from your peers when you go to work well attired. It does not have to be expensive clothing. There are lots of places we all know that sell inexpensive, good quality clothes. Keep your suit clean and ironed, shirt clean and ironed, and tucked in with tie (if required) worn properly. A belt, clean shoes and socks, preferably plain coloured (No Fred Flintstone or Spider Man socks; reserve those for the weekend or other social events). I know some of you who are reading this might disagree as you think you are a guru of fashion, the black Gok Wan or Alexander McQueen, but I'm sure that even they will tell you that its "style over fashion", especially in the work place. Black men, please take my advice and keep it simple with dark coloured suits, plain coloured socks, striped shirts – plain tie and plain shirts – striped or patterned tie. If you observe these simple rules, you will always look the part and make a big impression. Don't experiment with fashion in the work place; it can backfire. Remember, look the part that's above your current status in the organisation.

Don't smell "green!" Your personal hygiene is paramount. Too often, I'm speaking to black people with a body odour that is off-putting, and I'm speaking of both men and women. Just imagine being locked in a meeting room in a team meeting, and there is a really off-putting smell in this small meeting room; this breaks concentration and limits the team's ability to think, be innovative and come up with breakthrough solutions. Some persons might say that body odour is acceptable where they originate from and that in some cultures this is seen as a sign of great strength or even sexual attraction. Here again, I must point out that corporate norms are different from the social norms that I discussed earlier. In the workplace, this is unacceptable and leads to gossiping, ridicule and covert disrespect.

Most persons in an organisation will ignore the presence of your odour, hoping it will go away or that someone else will let you know. This leads to disruptions in the team dynamics and possibly the organisation. If you have a medical issue that results in the emitting of this kind of body odour, please speak to your doctor and see what can be done. Otherwise, you must have regular showers or baths, and use antiperspirant, or other accessories to help you get the smell under control.

If you are not sure whether or not you have a body odour, smell yourself regularly, especially your armpits, or ask one of your friends, and tell them you want an honest opinion. If the answer is yes, please, for heaven's sake, do something about it. It will boost your confidence and make you a much better person to work and collaborate with in the workplace.

Work Discipline

This is also an area of vast difference in terms of norms between the corporate world and the social norms of some black cultures. As black people, we seem to have an issue with time. I am sure you have heard the expression "not black people time or not African time or not black man time (BMT)". Not good! I will be the first to say I had this issue, and I have worked relentlessly over a period to correct this.

Being at work, or at meetings on time, and not giving continuous excuses for being late or "slagging off", is a key corporate behaviour that must be upheld and maintained. I can hear you thinking – that "slavery has been abolished"; and I would agree with you, but I have used the word "continuous". Being late occasionally is acceptable as unexpected things do occur. Trains run late, emergencies happen at home, or inclement weather issues, among other things, can result in us being late. What I am referring to here is perpetual lateness or tardiness. This behaviour is also reflected in the late submission of your task or deliverables and the related excuses which result in bad performance appraisals.

Yes, this might be a stereotypical view of black people, and you might say I am just reinforcing this argument of how we are viewed. But let us be honest here and admit that the issue does exist within our community. Having worked with and managed many black persons, I have had my share of having to deal with this issue. I mentor many "black bright sparks", and I also have this issue with some of them who turn up late for a session and give an excuse all the time. I usually tell those with this problem that if they do not improve, I will drop them from the mentoring circle. This is the same approach that will be taken towards this behaviour in the corporate world.

As a "black bright spark", delivering projects and tasks on time is paramount to your delivering phenomenal results leaving memorable experiences and climbing the corporate ladder. Develop the discipline of planning your task with enough buffer time to ensure there is time to take corrective action if something should go wrong. Meeting the deadline is key.

Having the discipline to avoid, stay away from, and desist from being drawn into office gossip and politics is also very essential. Office politics and gossip can be destructive to the team and to your prospect of winning in the corporate rat race. We all like a bit of gossip, but tread lightly, as those that gossip about others with you will gossip about you with others, embellishing what you said. Be warned. Stay clear!

The chameleon in you

Right or wrong, being a "black bright spark" in the corporate rat race is akin to being a chameleon. It's almost as if when you leave the confines of your home and the community in which you live, you need to change shades or colour, metaphorically speaking (not that this is possible for black people ☺) and adapt to the corporate world environment that you will be spending most of the day in. Conformity to the norms of the corporate world is not a bad thing, as it can lead to your learning, widening your knowledge and network. It is an invaluable part of the overall package for you to ultimately increase your net worth.

Our values, which are important to us, drive our normative actions. We constantly display our values every day. How you think about your body, for example, determines what you eat. The car you drive and the values you have about the environment, determines whether you purchase a hybrid car or an SUV. The way you dress tells a lot about your values. Do you have on an un-tucked shirt, messy hair, and sagging pants, or do you wear a buttoned-down collar, a blazer, and with hair well groomed? If you are often sarcastic in your comments, you might value humour in your social relationships, but if you are a person who is always polite you may place a higher priority on respect.

As a "black bright spark", you should get to know what your values are as well as the values of the company you work for. You can become disillusioned if the company's espoused values do not match its values-in-action. This kind of behaviour is called hypocrisy, and nobody likes a hypocrite; so you need to determine if this is a place for you to grow and succeed, or if you should take your talent and skills some place else. Values can be the foundation for norms; so, corporate norms are shaped and developed by the company's values. Norms are the attitudes and behaviours of the members of that organisation, and those values are what are important to those members.

If an organisation espouses that one of its values is equality, and yet, when you look at the senior management team, there are no women or persons of colour, then you have to wonder if this is a true value, and whether or not this is the organisation for you. Before I applied for any role or when being headhunted for a role, I usually research the prospective company to identify its values, principles, and the composition of its senior team. For me, it's important that the values of the prospective company are aligned somewhat to my values and beliefs and that it would be a place for me to learn, grow and enjoy working. I have turned down very lucrative roles for less paying ones because I felt the less paying role was in an organisation that better fit my values and aspirations. I place a high price on my values and beliefs because I am a strong go-getter with loads of confidence, experience and qualifications who is willing to disrupt the status quo to drive change for the better. I am also very entrepreneurial; so for my sanity's sake, I need to be in an organisation that will allow me to live and expand with these values.

Norms give a sense of shared values. The norms and values of any organisation define its culture, just as the norms and values of your race are part of your culture. Learn this and make it work to your advantage.

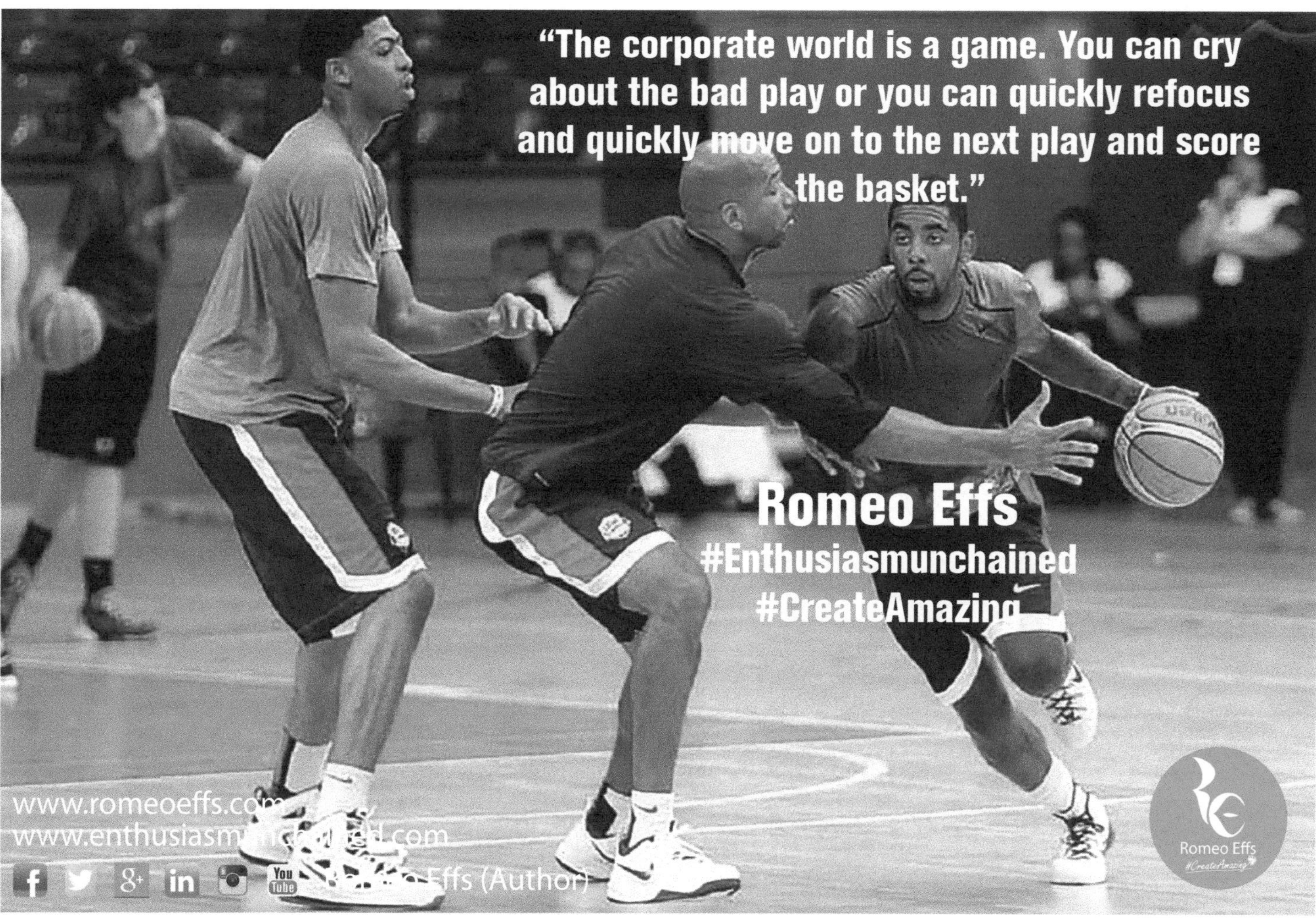
"The corporate world is a game. You can cry about the bad play or you can quickly refocus and quickly move on to the next play and score the basket."
Romeo Effs
#Enthusiasmunchained
#CreateAmazing
www.romeoeffs.com
Romeo Effs
#CreateAmazing

Please Listen & Watch
www.enthusiasmunchained.com/EU2

THREE

You Don't Have a Chip on Your Shoulder

A man is but a product of his thoughts; what he thinks he becomes

Mahatma Ghandi

When I first started working in corporate UK, and usually being the only black in the room, some of my colleagues would often say to me "we like working with you because you don't have a chip on your shoulder, or you are not the typical angry black male". I usually turned to look at my shoulder, sarcastically of course, to see what they are referring to, as I didn't understand why they would have thought that black males have an ego and anger problem.

Over the years, I have come to realise that this so called "chip that you have on your shoulder" should actually be more like a severed shoulder blade with all that I have observed Black people go through in the corporate world. But as a "bright black spark", you should not get yourself caught up in this and be concerned too much with this stereotypical mumbo jumbo, as it only serves to distract you from achieving your true goal and reaching your dangling carrot. Flip the script as I did, consider this chip to be your confidence, your drive for success, your certainty and your power of purpose and determination. Like an African Warrior, wear this chip with pride. Do not be arrogant and egotistical! There is a thin line between confidence and arrogance, so ensure the pendulum swings more to one side (confidence) than the other. Arrogance and ego have their place, but not in the corporate world.

Using a broad brush to paint us all…Not good!

I do acknowledge that some of us "black bright sparks" fit this stereotype. I am not here to deny any fact. But using the negative encounters that one has experienced, perhaps with one or two black persons, and then casting an assertion on an entire population is highly disconcerting and wrong. I have met and worked with a few in my career and have even had some in my mentoring circle. They usually see the corporate world from one perspective – either black or white. They view everything that happens to them in the work place as racism or a fight against them. You usually hear them make statements such as "they are racist in this place", "there is a glass ceiling", "they are holding me back", or "the white person will always get promoted". This kind of thinking is negative and defeatist, and as a "black bright spark" who knows what you want to achieve, this kind of thinking should be dumped permanently. When you feel yourself harbouring these thoughts, just refocus and think of your goals, dreams and objectives. No obstacle or barrier that forms against me shall prosper – say it and believe it, and you shall rise above it. Remind yourself that you are a born champion, can conquer it all, and you are the Michelangelo of your own life.

Then, there are those that make the pendulum swing so far to the side of self-importance (arrogance) and ego that they forget themselves. They might refuse to accept and see themselves as being black. They refuse to accept their culture and heritage and think that they are someone else, when they are not. They are usually extremely pompous and try to look or walk the other way whenever they see another black person approaching. I have also worked with some of these in my career, but I am quick to seek them out and point out in a respectful way the impact that their behaviour is usually having in the team. Sometimes their responses are positive, as they temper and balance it over time, while some ignore the advice and carry on. These individuals will sometimes make it and win in the corporate rat race, but most times, they don't. They either "burn out" from trying too hard at being someone they are not, and always having to push a loaded truck up a hill by themselves. They may "drop out", as travelling the corporate journey alone as a "black bright spark" can be lonely, tiring and weary. They "sell-out", real or perceived; continuing to believe that it's only they that matter. They can make it on their own without community support or giving back; the pendulum's now totally stationary in one extreme.

This kind of behaviour can usually stem from past experiences that this person has had, in which case it is harder to break this thought pattern, getting the pendulum to balance, and shift that mind-set. Someone I know was in this same position. He started as a graduate trainee in one of the larger oil companies. He worked really hard hitting all his targets. However, he was always overlooked for progression. He was talking to a friend about this, just trying to get some insight as to what was wrong. The friend told him that he was being discriminated against and that it was institutionalised racism. He started harbouring thoughts of this and saw everything in the work place through these lenses. He became critical of everything that was said to him, and every advice, good or bad, he took as being destructive criticism (racist) and that he was being fought against. He started pushing back real hard to the point of being disrespectful and undermining his team. When HR spoke to him about his behaviour, as a result of the complaints they were receiving, he filed racial complaints against members of his team.

Someone who worked with this person asked me to have a talk with him, as they saw him as a "black bright spark" that was losing his way. I found out that in the department he worked there were a number of competencies that he needed to complete before he could be considered for progression. I inquired as to why he did not complete the competencies for progression. His response was his workload, and that he had seen others progress without completing the competencies because they were white. Poor excuse! How can you complain when you have not done what is required for you to progress? It's the corporate policy and norm that in order to progress, there is a path you need to follow. Don't get caught up with what has happened to others. You don't know their circumstances. I have flown past many promotional steps because I have a Master's degree, or because I have done an external executive course, so I was exempted. After pointing out all this and some other possibilities, I got him to begin to realise that he had the wrong approach and that he needed to look at and work on his own mind-set. It was only after this "light bulb" moment that he told me how his friend planted this destructive seed in his head. As a result of his behaviour, he had become isolated in the work place; no one wanted to work with him even though he was good at what he does. They felt they might say something wrong, resulting in him lashing out at them or filing an official complaint. This isolation even drove this notion of "them" vs. "me" even deeper into his sub-consciousness, which created stress, illness and a lack of trust for his peers. It is easy to see how this kind of behaviour can destroy someone with real potential and also result in his fellow team members using a broad brush to paint all "bright black spark" as angry and bitter. I encouraged him to get the competencies and to rebuild trust amongst his colleagues by volunteering to work on a few of the charity fundraising projects the company runs, and possibly go on some of the team outings. He will need to take baby steps to get back on track, rebond with the corporate norms, and regain his colleagues' trust. Although it will be a long road ahead, this is a career he wants, and a company he wants to be in.

The "Anger" in the angry black man

This *so called* "anger" in you real or perceived is an innate belief and a burning desire to succeed. It is what gives you as a "bright black spark" the power of purpose and determination to drive and push with all your zeal and zest towards that dream or goal you have set for yourself. Never lose this *so called* "anger". Instead channel it inwards and use it as a driving force to propel you and to remind you of where you are coming from, where you want to be, and what you want to accomplish. Never let it control you, your respect of others, your values, and most importantly, your professionalism. You are the master of your thoughts and actions; so control this emotion, and don't let it control you. We are a very emotional people, when we cry, we holler. When we are angry we lash out hard, when we laugh we do it loud and proud. But this *so called* "Anger" we have to learn to control and use it as tool and device for positive growth, development and upward mobility.

As "black bright sparks", we need to learn early in the game the importance of confidence, self-esteem, and the need to balance this with ego and self-importance. "Black bright sparks" are usually intelligent, well read and well educated. We are usually natural leaders at the forefront of most things in our school, university, communities, and even at work.

We are or were president of one or two societies, clubs or organisations, and trustees of charities. We may also have or will start a few charities, volunteered in our communities, active in our churches, or other places of worship, active politically, be trade union members or engaged in some other kind of activity which raised our profile and level of importance amongst our peers. People usually describe you as an over-achiever, a leader or in my case, they usually describe me as being "nuff", which is a Jamaican term, with its roots in enough (plentiful), for always being involved, being upfront or having a commanding and colourful presence. Frankly – a "black bright spark". With all of that happening, there can be the tendency for arrogance (self-importance) and ego to slip in and take over. It's important to recognise this, quickly rebalance and stay grounded.

Success comes in many packages, shapes, and sizes; there is no one-size-fits-all as far as success is concerned. You need to determine what success looks and feels like to you and use all this energy to muster and propel yourself there. Having role models is good; and aspiring to achieve what they have is also good, but only if that is what you really and truly believe that you want. Success is abundant, it has no limitations, no boundaries, no glass ceilings, and so should your dreams. Aspire to achieve bigger and better things than those whom you admire and those who inspire you, if that is what you want, and use this energy, the "black man anger" always and only inwards to get you there.

Don't lose your focus; it becomes your story and determines your actions

This talk of an angry black man with a chip on his shoulder, while real as I have stated before, is a false generalisation.

Those who use this "anger" externally as a defensive mechanism to ward off the "evil" of the workplace will soon find out that they either remain in the same place all their lives, wondering why they have not achieved their goals, or are constantly fighting a battle that is draining and tiresome. They will see other "black bright sparks" flying at knots speed, pass them in the workplace, achieving their full potential, making lots of money, and enjoying the finer things in life. If they don't realise that this mind set is what's holding them back, and make a drastic shift, rebalancing the pendulum, they will have to settle for second best or no place at all.

So, as a "black bright spark", decide on what you are going to focus on. Have a tunnel vision approach when focusing, so that you zoom in and see clearly what your purpose, values, mission and vision is, as this can help you map out your journey to success writing your "Story". I am sure you can remember when you were a child, and you dreamt of becoming an astronaut or a fireman, a doctor or a judge. You imagined it, and it was clear and vivid. That is the kind of visual focus that you need to have and maintain each day to make your dream a reality.

When you are in the stage of tunnel vision on your dream, it is also key to focus on what you currently have. Where are you now in this grand scheme of achieving this dream? Realise and accept your current position, and then plan the steps towards getting there. (I will deal with this more in Chapter 6).

Focus on what you can control; its wasted energy to focus on things outside your control. Use this energy to control, develop, and grow those things that you can influence. You cannot control what people think or say about you, but with time and by your actions, you can influence it. Focus on becoming a high performer; that, you have total control of, and watch the way in which people perceive you and think of your change.

Focus on your purpose, and vision for the future. Keep your purpose and the vision of what you want to be and to accomplish in the forefront of your mind, your "dangling carrot". Never lose this vision outside your head. You should eat, sleep, walk and talk with this vision being central to your thoughts. This obsession with your purpose and vision will determine your state of mind and your state of being. It is what I call your "State". Your "State" includes the feelings, emotions, values and beliefs system that you are prepared to use and act upon to do and to make your vision a reality.

Your focus and state of mind determines your story. Your story is the blue print of how you will achieve your goal. It's the roadmap to your vision, underlined by your purpose and your belief system. Your "Story" is the planned steps required on your success journey. Your "Story" determines and lays out clearly what your vision is, how you plan to get there (the roadmap). It helps you to anticipate obstacles you might experience, as well as the people and resources you will need along the way.

> Your "Story" drives and determines the actions you take, what you will do, and how you will do it to achieve your vision.

I have developed a 4-step methodology that I use with those I mentor and coach to help them better succeed by concentrating on these four areas – Focus = State = Story = Actions (FSSA). I call it the R.E. Success Quadrant ™ or RESQ ™ (pronounced 'Rescue'), depicted below.

This is a powerful tool that will help you to determine your true-life's purpose, values and vision. Realign your state. Write a roadmap for your vision and provide tools for taking the right action.

> I invite you to visit *www.romeoeffs.com* and try these interactive tools.

I will be referring to these four elements throughout the rest of the book as I use them to "salt and pepper" different points.

Anticipation is the ultimate power of success

One of the ways I anticipate outcomes of any decision I make or will be making is to envision the possible outcome and the rippling effects such a decision will have on my objective and my team. I love sports, and basketball is one of my favourite games. Basketball, like many other sports, is about anticipating your opponents' moves and putting the play in place to prevent them from making that move towards the basket. You have to be swift and powerful, both physically and mentally, and mitigate the plays so that you are the one that scores and takes your team to victory.

As a "black bright spark", it is similar in the corporate world. Those "black bright sparks" that have succeeded in the corporate rat race were able to anticipate and know how the clock was ticking and how the corporate game was being played and was moving. The ability to do this is something you have to learn, constantly develop, and nurture.

R.E SUCCESS QUADRANT

RESQ™

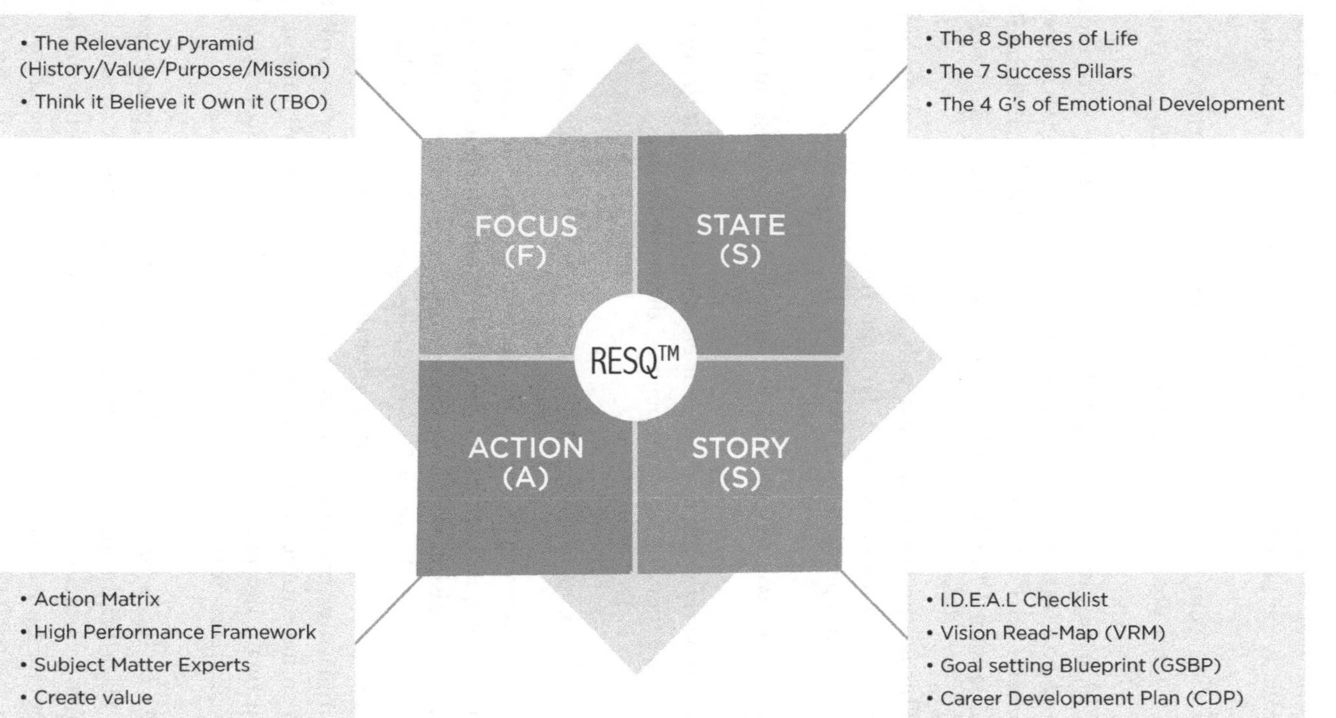
• The Relevancy Pyramid (History/Value/Purpose/Mission)
• Think it Believe it Own it (TBO)
• The 8 Spheres of Life
• The 7 Success Pillars
• The 4 G's of Emotional Development
FOCUS (F)
STATE (S)
RESQ™
ACTION (A)
STORY (S)
• Action Matrix
• High Performance Framework
• Subject Matter Experts
• Create value
• I.D.E.A.L Checklist
• Vision Read-Map (VRM)
• Goal setting Blueprint (GSBP)
• Career Development Plan (CDP)

One way of doing this is to learn from those who have done it before you. Seek them out, speak to them, and ask for their advice. Learn from their journey, and their stories, good or bad. Give yourself the benefit of leveraging the success of others to help you on your success journey. No one is self-made! I have had the privilege of having numerous mentors, coaches and advisors throughout my career. Some genuinely wanted to help. Some only accept the title because it gives them status in the organisation. Some made no time to see me, no matter how often I booked time in their diaries or asked to catch up. Each of these, I took as a learning experience as they all had different impacts. Keep looking until you find one that genuinely cares about your success and wants to help.

The ability to visualise outcomes and mitigate or plan around those that might have a negative impact on our story is crucial. Learn from your experiences and the experience of others, but that is all; learn and move on. Use it to change your state in a positive way, so you can write the best story and take decisive action accordingly towards your dreams and your goals.

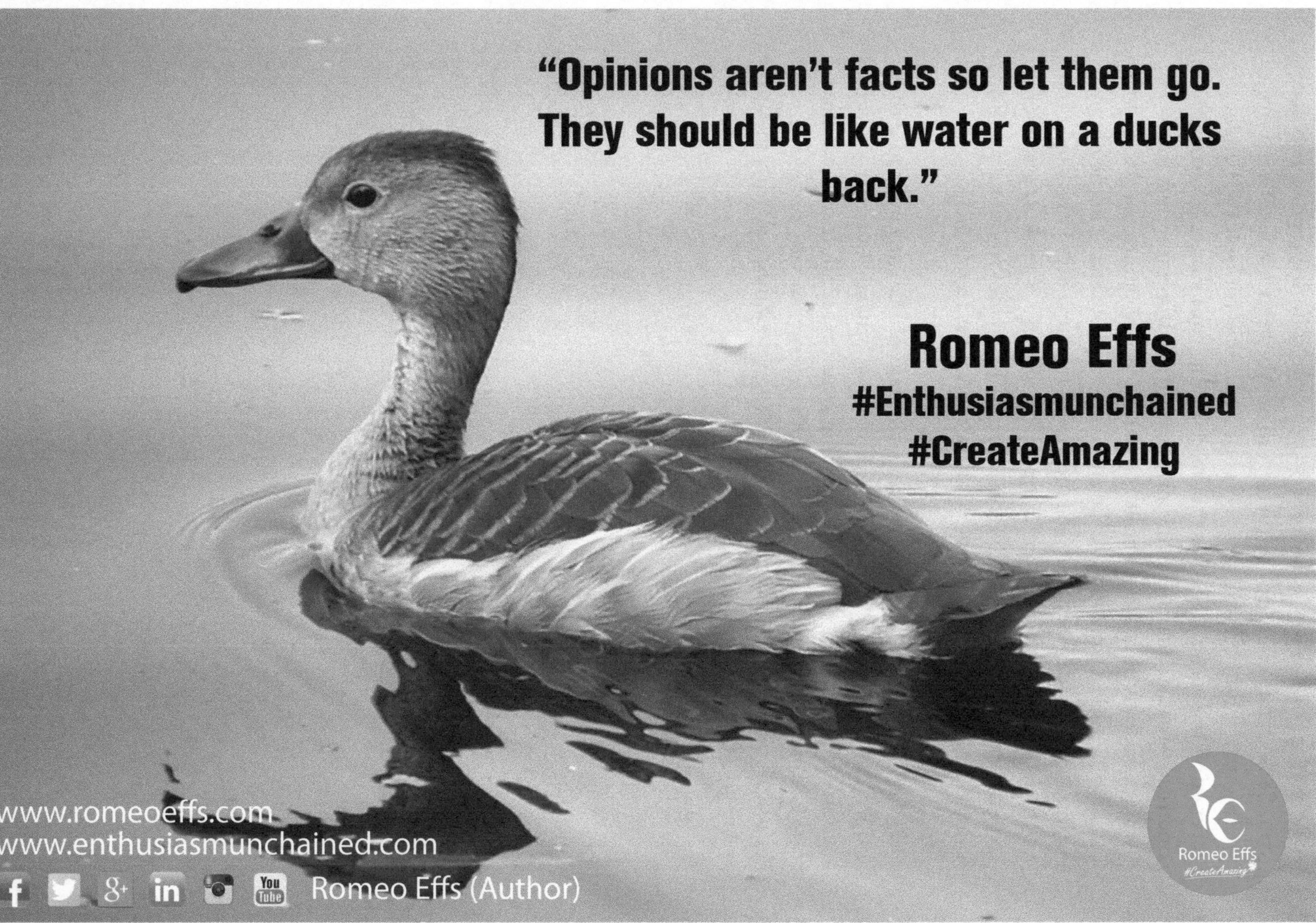
"Opinions aren't facts so let them go.
They should be like water on a ducks
back."
Romeo Effs
#Enthusiasmunchained
#CreateAmazing
www.romeoeffs.com
www.enthusiasmunchained.com
Romeo Effs (Author)
Romeo Effs
#CreateAmazing

Please Listen & Watch
www.enthusiasmunchained.com/EU3

FOUR

"RACISM": THAT IS SO 1980S; GET OVER IT!

"People fail to get along because they fear each other; they fear each other because they don't know each other; they don't know each other because they have not communicated with each other".

"The Arc of the Moral Universe Is Long, but It Bends Toward Justice".

MARTIN LUTHER KING JR.

Racism is real; that's a fact

I have always been proud of myself growing up in a country (Jamaica) where racism does not exist. I had as much and as equal an opportunity to become successful as any other person. I am not saying that there were no poor persons in this society and that the division between rich and poor was not significant; but through education, many escaped the boundaries of their "social class" and elevated themselves to great success. It was not ever "racism", but what I call "classism". It is this upbringing that has caused me to view the issue of racism in the corporate world in countries such as The UK & USA through different lenses.

I know that some of you reading this might be thinking that I am a mad man that does not know what he is talking about, and that I did not live the experiences of your lives in the seventies, and eighties when this was way more prevalent. And you may be right that I did not live in the UK or the USA during those times, but what I have experienced and achieved as a black man over the last eight years in corporate UK is testament that you don't have to be a "sell out" to get to a senior position in some of the most well-known and profitable FTSE companies in the UK and Globally. I have only had one experience in my UK Corporate Career that I would classify as being racist, and I only classified it as such when I was told by another senior colleague that it was. I treat these things like "water on a duck's back"; it will always run off. I think of and treat people who think they can make racist comments towards me or use racist tactics to prevent me from getting to my goal as idiots, (or as they say in Jamaica – eediat), as being behind the times and an ill-mannered fool. I usually put them in their place by letting them know how I feel in no uncertain terms, but in a polite, respectful, diplomatic and professional manner. People who are still racist in the corporate world in this day and age have driven well past the last exit to relevance and will soon realise that they will become extinct. It's not a matter of, 'if' more people of colour will take the helm of some of these global conglomerates; it's a matter of 'when". At the time of writing this book (2013), there were 50 Billionaires in Africa and more and more of the global black population is getting educated, starting their own business and out-stripping their counterparts in the corporate world. From what I can see, it will be sooner rather than later.

The incident I refer to earlier happened in my early years as a Senior Manager in the UK. In this company four Senior Managers shared one Executive Assistant (EA). I was on a call and needed to get some urgent information from the shared EA. All the offices had glass half way up, so I was able to look across, and spot her in the office of another Senior Manager. I went to the office door, which was opened, pushed my head in and said excuse me, Joshua (not real name), can you excuse Karen (not real name) for a minute? I need her to give me some information urgently for a client who I am on a conference call with. Joshua got up without even saying a word and slammed the door shut in my face. At the time, I did not see this as being racist and even now I struggle to see it as such because of how and where I was brought up. I was outraged, but calm. I opened the door, stepped in his office, and closed the door behind me. I could see total fear in his face as if he thought I was going to slap him into eternity. I calmly looked him in the eyes and told him in no uncertain terms that where I am from and in my culture, if you need privacy, the correct and respectful way to do it was to say "excuse me, but I need some privacy right now, would you mind coming back in a few minutes". I continued to advise that he should take some time to learn and cultivate some "manners" and respect for others, regardless of his status in the organisation. I told him he was out-of-order, rude, and obviously had forgotten the basic manners and principles that I knew his parents taught him. I also told him that he should learn from his mistake and never let another incident as such occur to anyone else in the organisation. I then proceeded to tell our shared EA what I needed and that I would appreciate if she acted on it immediately, to which she complied.

I never repeated the details of the incident to anyone else as I thought it was dealt with; and once I had spoken to him about how I felt, I had moved on. However, the EA relayed this to others in the organisation. Two weeks later, I happened to be in the lift with the UK Managing Director. He referred to me by name (which I was totally surprised at), commented, and congratulated me for dealing with the incident in a professional manner. He remarked that those types of racist behaviours are not tolerated within the organisation and that he had instructed HR to investigate and deal with the instigator. I informed him that at no time had I thought of the incident as being racist, but rather one of disrespect and ill-mannered behaviour. Joshua apologised, and we went on to have a mutually respectful working relationship until I left the company. In this whole situation, was I being naïve or was I being pragmatic?

I made a conscious decision not to get drawn into this race blame culture and "racism tornado". Yes, there are fewer "black bright sparks" in senior roles within corporate UK. Yes, the latest study by Business in the Community Campaign Race for Opportunity shows that over 50% of all black males between 18 and 27 is unemployed in London (2012). But on the bright side, we are bucking the trend and even greater numbers of black pupils are graduating from universities, with a larger portion of them starting their own business or getting corporate roles. What we need to teach these "black bright sparks" is how to play the corporate game to win in the corporate rat race. In generations to come, this will not be an issue in corporate UK. What we need to understand and accept, to paraphrase Dr. Martin Luther King, Jr., is that the arch of morality is long and bends slowly, but it bends towards fairness and justice for all. If we look back to the seventies and eighties and compare that time to the corporate world today, I am sure you will see some positive steps that all of us have taken.

There is much more work to be done, I agree, to level the playing field; hence, one of the reasons for writing this book. As "black bright sparks", we should not, however, let this issue of racism consume our energies and serve as a distraction to achieving our goals. We should not use "racism" as an excuse for not realising our full potential or achieving our goals. We should not use "racism" as a hindrance or shield from becoming tunnel-visioned, but rather as a focus for our purpose, to build a compelling story, which in turn drives our state of mind and emotion to take inspired action. Racism is just another mechanism to get us off track and keep us "in our place", causing us to be fearful. Fearful of success, fearful of the organisation, fearful of taking risks and bolstering that inner critic that prevents us from taking bold action to be a phenomenal success and leave a legacy in this world. Yes, racism does exist in corporate UK; just be aware of it, but do not let it consume your thoughts to the point that it saps or eliminates your power of purpose and determination for becoming someone great and #CreateAmazing.

History can be your friend or your worst enemy

Those who might criticise my stance on racism in the corporate world may well point to history. As a lover of history, though by no means a historian, I do believe that history, if not taken into context, read and interpreted in the era that it happened can be fatal in today's world. We just need to look at all the major conflicts happening throughout the world to see how history has played a damning part in these destructive affairs. I have always held the view that history is just that "history", the past. It is important to know your past as I have said before, and understand that as black people or people of colour, we are from a line of empire builders, inventors, and great world leaders, known and unknown. We should use history only as a guide to shape our focus in a positive way, not as a determinate factor.

As "black bright sparks", we must learn to "stand on the shoulders of giants", seek out those great thinkers and achievers who have gone before us, learn from them and use them as motivators to achieve even greater success. However, there comes a time when we need to step off their shoulders, stepping even higher to leave you lasting memorable experiences, your change and your own legacy.

As "black bright sparks", you must understand that while you may speak or write your way into a role, job or task, that only performance will keep you there and keep you moving. The only way we can change our status, position, or circumstances in the corporate world is by achievements. One of the mottos I live by is that change is measured by achievements, not by words and speeches. Use our history to influence this change, leave a legacy for others to emulate as part of history, and change the way we are perceived by others as black people. Remember performance knows no colour.

Keep it real

Racism in the work place is illegal; there are strict laws against this kind of behaviour, such as the Equalities Act 2010 in the UK and the Civil Rights Act 1991 in the USA, to name a few. Most companies also have an equalities policy or statement and will act if they are told about racist behaviour in the work place. However, as most black persons in corporate will tell you, institutional racism is covert and subtle whenever it is practised.

As a "black bright spark", you have a choice. You are bright, intelligent, and gifted; you don't have to tolerate any form of action that will demotivate, distract or hinder your progress. Walk away and find somewhere new to shine. Somewhere where your talents and skills will be appreciated and valued for what they really are. There are many companies in the corporate world like this. Challenge yourself by trusting yourself, and you will be amazed to find how easy it is to find that right place.

The other option, if you believe you are at the right company, and you really love what you do, is to speak out in a respectful, non-aggressive, calm, and professional manner. Let others know how you feel and what you observe as being wrong with the situation; but more importantly, let the perpetrator know how you feel and that such behaviour and conduct will not be tolerated. Remember, do it in a professional and respectful manner. Sometimes, it's even best to send this to the person(s) in writing. Just know that as a "black bright spark", you are a champion, and so you have the potential to deliver this message in a way that it will be received as being professional and non-judgemental.

The most important thing, which I cannot overemphasise, is not to allow this corporate or institutional racism tornado that people seem to talk so much about and seem to think exists in magnitude, to overtake your thoughts, feelings and emotions in such a way that it dims your spark. I have seen too many people "burn out" and not achieve their full potential and their dreams because they get too consumed in fighting a losing battle of discrimination, trying to prove to themselves and the world that they can win. The only consolation I have had over the years in dealing with this and which I pass on to the "black bright sparks" that I mentor and coach is that as a race, we shall overcome this too, like so many other struggles we have endured. As my dear granny would say "time is the master of everything, so leave it to time". So, if you think you can win that discrimination claim and affect lasting change, go for it and shout loud. If you feel overwhelmed, battered and bruised, walk away, and find that new vibrant place to shine, focus and attain your dreams and goals. Learn to choose your battles, and as I have always practiced, only choose the ones you know you have a greater advantage of winning.

Use racism as a driving force to propel you to succeed

I have always believed and practised the notion of what I call "positive retribution". Positive retribution is where I prove people wrong when they tell me I cannot do or achieve something, or when they say it's impossible to do. If you want me to push harder and to move mountains, tell me that I cannot do or accomplish something. I have noticed this about myself since I was a child, and it has worked positively for me so far. If there are, however, compelling facts that are put forward to show that it is going to be impossible to accomplish this task in the way I propose, then, of course, I will reconsider, and when necessary, concede. In most of the cases, however, it becomes a compelling drive to make it happen, just to prove the cynics wrong.

I am a strong believer that whatever the mind of man conceives and believes, it can achieve. I ask my mentees to believe this and use it as a mantra in conceiving and conceptualising their vision. When it comes to this issue of racism, the best thing we as "black bright sparks" and indeed black people can do is to take positive revenge. We need to prove to the corporate "naysayers" that they are wrong, by becoming great business leaders, achieving phenomenal results, accomplishing things that have never been thought of before and becoming extraordinarily successful. Make sure that it's seen and felt so that it cannot be denied. Prove people wrong when they try to deliberately prevent you from achieving your goals. Sometimes, you might have to take a step back to take two or three steps forward, but sometimes that is the sacrifice you will have to make to reach your vision. With this steely power of purpose and determination, I focused on becoming an empire builder, including everything that comes with it. Develop that tunnel vision approach towards your vision, your story, and your success journey.

Stop believing in this institutional racism and glass ceiling phenomena and mumbo jumbo; become resourceful and find a way around it, as if it does exists and become that champion of industry, that thought leader, that subject matter expert, and that successful, great and inspirational individual you were born to be. Racist opinions aren't facts, they are platitudinous drivel, and so let them go. Let them be like water off a duck's back that flows off without getting your skin wet. Don't let it penetrate your psyche, as it can slow you down and drag you into a fight that is not winnable. Be aware it exists, and manoeuvre your way around it, through it, and over it, to accomplish that which you know and believe you can become.

The way I view racism in the corporate world is that it is the problem of those that practise and condone it. It is not my problem, so I am not going to allow it to weigh me down and slow my speed to success. I don't want or need that unwanted baggage, so I am not taking it aboard my flight to success. Hopefully, after reading the tips and ideas in this book you will find a path to do just this.

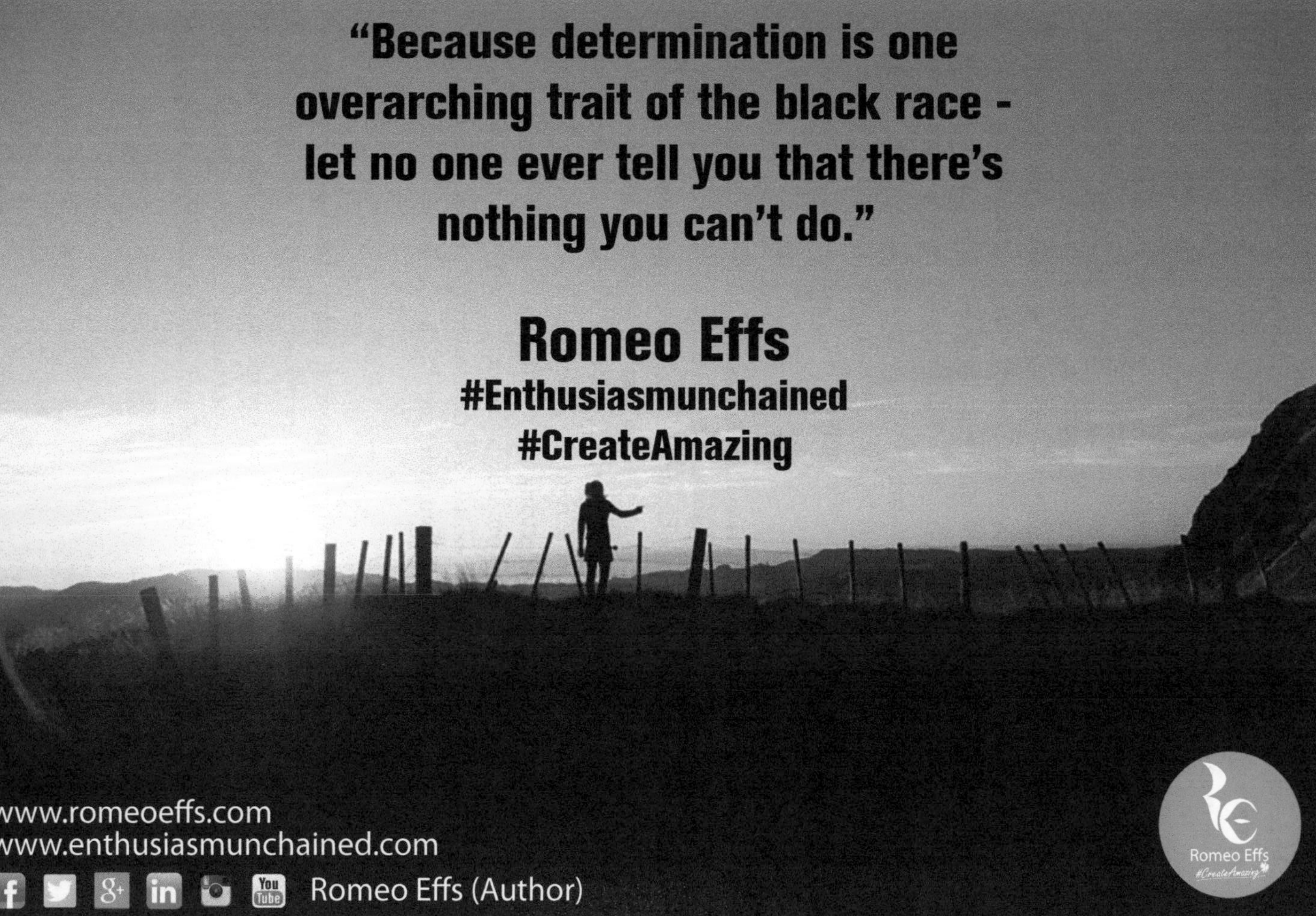
"Because determination is one
overarching trait of the black race -
let no one ever tell you that there's
nothing you can't do."
Romeo Effs
#Enthusiasmunchained
#CreateAmazing
www.romeoeffs.com
www.enthusiasmunchained.com
Romeo Effs (Author)
Romeo Effs
#CreateAmazing

Please Listen & Watch
www.enthusiasmunchained.com/EU4

FIVE

DON'T LIMIT YOUR POTENTIAL BY DIMINISHING YOUR GLOW

I learned that courage was not the absence of fear, but the triumph over it. The brave man is not he who feels afraid but he that conquers that fear.

NELSON MANDELA
1ST BLACK PRESIDENT OF SOUTH AFRICA

I was on my way home one afternoon and spotted some guys putting up a huge billboard. I spotted the words 'potential', and was intrigued. I waited until they had completed putting all parts of the billboard together and a smile came across my face. The billboard read: Potential…Delivered. On one side it had a rough diamond with the words "Potential", and on the other side, it had a glistening diamond with the words "delivered" next to it.

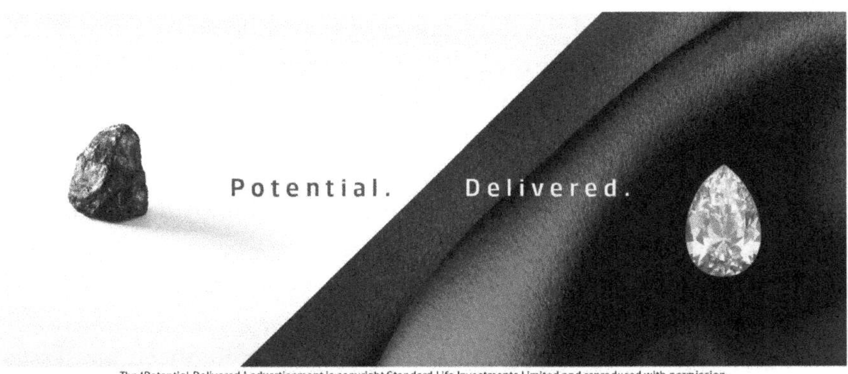

The 'Potential.Delivered.' advertisement is copyright Standard Life Investments Limited and reproduced with permission.

I smiled, shook my head, and walked off as I have always thought of every single one of my mentees and of all "black bright sparks" in this way, a diamond in the rough. They have such passion and desire to succeed and all that is required is to put them through that process of believing in themselves and applying a mechanism and process for achieving their goals. We all have that inborn drive and tenacity to achieve phenomenal things. It does not matter what our status in life is, where we live, which school we attended, whether we have a degree or not, what our background, race or tribe is; we can achieve greatness. It's in all of us. There are many who have achieved phenomenal success and who have come from one or more of these circumstances, but what differentiated them was their "power of purpose and determination". They were hungry for success. Are you hungry for success?

Some "Black bright sparks" tend to diminish their glow and fail in most instances because of "blame" and "excuses". They blame the past and the impact of slavery, colonisation and being taken from the motherland, and all that was inflicted on us as a people. They blame the government for not doing enough to force employers to promote us and put quotas in place for "ethnic minorities" on boards and in senior management.

Yet some of you are not prepared to do what it takes to perform at this level. You blame your parents for not pushing you enough in school and at home, and for not setting the examples, and giving you the values you need. You blame your teachers in school for telling you that you were not good enough, and for encouraging you to choose a career you did not want or see yourself doing. You envy and blame others because they have achieved and can afford the finer things in life while you are struggling financially. Yet, we all have the ability to make our own choices using our brain (considered to be the most powerful machine on earth), to think, influence, make decisions and take action to change our circumstances.

Some of you find "excuses" for your procrastination to decide to take action, to changing your state and building a more compelling story for success.

I was speaking to a "black bright spark" who is an engineer, and I was telling him that I was writing a book about the struggles of black people in corporate UK. He was happy that this issue was being taken on, but he began lamenting that as a black engineer, it was different. He believed that those who hired engineers had set a quota for the number of black engineers in industry, and more so, the numbers of black senior engineers. He believes that because this is set there was no way he could become a senior engineer in the firm he is working in and has just settled to being in the comfort of where he is and has been for the past 10 years. He also blamed the other senior black engineers that have been able to penetrate the so called "glass ceiling" for not doing enough to help other black engineers to do the same. Blah, blah, blah…I am really tired of hearing all these lame excuses from "black bright sparks" with big potential.

This kind of thinking and subsequent action diminishes your glow; and in some instances, extinguishes it altogether if there is not a significant mind shift. I asked, what was his career goal, and where he had envisioned himself in five to ten years after he had completed his engineering degree. His response was to own his own engineering firm, but he needed to develop a successful career rising to the level of a senior engineer before he could do that. I told him that they were not dependent, as I have known others who have started their own engineering firms without getting to a senior level in a large firm and that I know they are well respected and a "key person of influence" in their industry. I asked what steps (actions) he had taken over the past ten years towards either vision of achieving the status of Senior Engineer or owning his own firm. His remark was that he had been working hard and doing what he needed to do. That is excellent, but as a "black bright spark", the truth is that it is just not good enough. You need a plan or roadmap. Just working hard is not good enough. You have to be working hard towards something, some vision, some goal, and some purpose, with some form of plan or roadmap on how to get there.

This is something else we just need to accept and deal with, and see it as another obstacle that we need to overcome if we are to succeed and attain that vision we set for ourselves. I started asking him if he had done any refresher courses, attended any conferences or seminars, written any articles or volunteered for any projects outside of his area. Had he asked for an internal mentor or sponsor who is senior in the organisation, or even discussed with his boss his aspirations within the organisation and asked for help in getting there? The response was "No". Then, if you have not taken any action, how can you complain and what gives you the audacity to blame?

I pulled the napkin that was on the table we were sitting, and started mapping out the necessary actions he needed to take in order to get that senior level engineering experience he believes is required to give him the needed knowledge he thinks he needs to achieve his goal of owning his own firm. Notice I said "experience" as he does not necessarily have to be promoted to a senior level in his firm to get the experience. There are "many ways to skin a cat" as my Granny would say. Become resourceful; there is always, always, a way.

No more excuses

The only barrier to achieving your full potential, your goals and dreams is YOU. Stop being a "doubting Thomas", always doubting your ability and your greatness. Stop listening to those inner critics that always seem to find an excuse or reason for you not taking that bold action. Manage that inner critic by "laughing at it", and tell it that he does not know what you are about and is just a fool. You may also kill this inner critic, dismiss it immediately, and refrain from listening to it or you can "argue with it" until you get your way. Whatever way you find best to manage your inner critic, do it so it does not overtake your decision points. I prefer to "kill it", but that is just my preference.

Stop listening to what "naysayers" and negative people say. I have a simple philosophy of only surrounding myself with 90% positive people. Some negative people are family, so it's hard to shacke them off or get rid of them, while some help to keep you grounded. I am not saying that criticisms are not to be tolerated and are all bad. There is "constructive criticism", and there is "destructive criticism", and sometimes it is hard to distinguish one from the other.

Just for clarification: – constructive criticism examines what has gone wrong with the task or action and gives suggestions to improve the next time around. It highlights what exactly went wrong, examines the "behaviour" only, and not the personal traits of the person who carried out the action. It builds you up and reprimands or criticises you, but leaves your dignity

(Ok-ness) as a person intact. You should give yourself constructive criticism all the time. Destructive criticism, on the other hand, attacks your character, value and self-worth, blaming you for the failure, rather than the behaviour. It attacks and makes you become defensive and hostile.

If you keep on finding excuses, then you will find yourself in 10 years' time in the same place or lower, with the same dream. I discussed in Chapter 3, the notion RESQ (RE Success Quadrants) and the four quadrants: – FOCUS = STATE = STORY = ACTION. If you find out that you have taken action and are doing something to reach those goals, but you are not hitting those milestones, change your strategy, refocus and rewrite your story, and your roadmap. Change what you are doing, or how you are doing it. Ask yourself some riveting questions and be brutally honest with the answers. There is no need to lie to YOUR-SELF!

1. Did I do, or am I doing enough?
2. Did I follow what I said I would be doing?
3. What were the anticipated outcomes that I predicted (positive and negative)?
4. Did any of these materialise?

Don't keep doing the same thing repeatedly and expect a different result. If you plant an orange seed, don't expect to reap mangos. Change your strategy. Simplicity is the key; make and keep it simple and in small bite-sized chunks. Achieve and build up those small wins in preparation for that "quantum leap". When you change your strategy, ensure it fits your story or the rewritten version of the story. Anticipate the possible outcomes and have plans to mitigate and then take corrective action.

The universe has an abundance of resources. There is enough time in the day, there is enough money, and there are plenty of resources. So, stop using this as an excuse for not taking action and becoming great. Become resourceful; be innovative and creative with your ideas, and have that power of purpose and determination to get it done. There is an old African proverb that my Granny used to say: "for dry wood to blaze, it must seek fire".

When I was in university doing my first degree, I could not find the money to pay my tuition, and I was on the verge of being kicked out of university. I was totally distraught but always believed and had faith that I would find a way to pay the fees and complete my degree with honours. The university, at the time, had a number of guest lecturers that would fly into the island every week to give lectures and fly back out. I approached the university with a proposal that I could pick up these lecturers and charge less than what they were being charged, and they could put sixty per cent of my invoice towards covering my tuition while the balance paid to me would be needed to cover gas, etc. for the car. I did not even have a car of my own then, so I borrowed a car, initially, to do the run for a small fee which I paid out of the forty-five per cent I got from each invoice, until I was able to get a car on hire purchase from a car dealer. I delivered such exceptional service – juice and water on arrival, and sometimes a sandwich and fruit plate, which I made myself. I was always on time (well, most of the time ☺), provided baggage service, flight tracking for delays, etc., and pre check-in at the airport and hotel. The feedback to the university was top class, and soon they began asking me to take lecturers and other board members on trips. I then started getting referrals into embassies, and other companies. Within one year, I was able to pay off my second and third year university fees and started collecting full payments from the university, which had now crept back up to what they used to pay originally. This was the beginning of my third company VIP Car Services, which operated and grew successfully until I sold it in 2005.

Resourcefulness has no bounds. Think wide, think deep and most importantly, think like there are no boundaries and no barriers to you achieving what you have set out to achieve. I am a strong believer that the universe has an abundance of resources, and if you believe and have faith, it will deliver what you want and desire once you take the action it prompts you to take. I have proven it time and time again in my life, and I encourage those I work with and mentor to do the same, and they have seen great results. If you are resourceful enough, you will find the resources you need to get things done. Just be creative, fearless, innovative, and bold. Believe, have faith, and go after it with power of purpose and determination, and you will see how resources come flowing your way. So, no more excuses; take action now. I repeat: NO MORE EXCUSES; TAKE ACTION NOW!

Belief and Faith

I will expand on this later in Chapter 9 – but in order to succeed you have to Think It; Believe It; Own It (TBO). Have belief and unwavering faith in your dreams and goals.

When I speak of belief and faith, many will say "here we go again with the religious chant", but far from it. Those of us who are more spiritual will understand that belief and faith are not confined to the religious realm, but can be applied and is, in fact, applied more broadly. Ask anyone who has achieved great things or something of great significance, no matter how small, and hear what they tell you. They will always say things like..."I always knew I would do it"...or "I always believed I would get there". It is this "always know" that is the faith. Once you have identified your purpose and visualised your vision, you will get a feeling deep in your gut that makes you feel good. It will put a smile on your face and make you feel bubbly inside. That is the "always know" feeling. That is the accepting that you know it's possible. That is the believing that it can be done. That is the faith! So, when you start doubting yourself or having fear of failure and despair, go back to that thought and get that feeling. Use it as the inspiration, the driving force, and the propeller you need to get moving and keep moving. As Anthony Robbins would say, "emotion equals motion". If you have the right mental attitude (STATE), you can unleash your full potential.

As a "black bright spark", believing in your vision, having this "know I can do it" (faith) attitude, and trusting in your potential is the biggest advantage you can give yourself. It is no use having a vision and not believing in it and your potential to achieve it. Having a vision without faith is like an airplane flying aimlessly without a destination. It will soon run out of fuel and fall from the sky. So many great world and life-changing ideas die with people because of a lack of belief and faith in them. Don't let this happen to you!

Anything is possible and can be achieved if you put your mind, body and soul into it. As children, we had visions and dreams without limits, and some of those dreams have now become reality. You did not think how you were going to achieve it, become it, make it or break it. You just visualised it, and you believed in your soul it could happen. This is the kind of belief and blind faith you need to have in your vision, goals and dreams. Don't worry how you are going to get there; just know you will get there.

Look at some of the movies from the 70s and 80s, and you will see what was once a vision in a script is now reality. This vision in script was someone's idea. A prime example is Star Trek, (yes, I am a Trekkie), where they used to have tablets and mobile phones, and fly in space ships across the galaxy. We now have thousands of different tablets and mobile phones, and after Richard Branson is done with us, I'm sure we will be jetting across the Galaxy in one of his space ships. I am sure when Sir Richard Branson came up with the idea of taking tourists into space, that there were people saying it could not be done. He had a vision, he believed in it and "always knew" (faith) that it could and would be done. If you read Sir Richard Branson's story (someone whom I really admire), you will see that throughout his life he had a purpose and vision (FOCUS), had the right mind set (STATE), knew what he wanted to achieve (STORY) and made it happen with a good team (ACTION).

Everyday a new star or galaxy is discovered, and each time I read about another new discovery, I think about each "black bright spark" that is born; yet to be discovered. Your parents always had the biggest ambitions for you and always hoped that you would achieve great things. As a parent myself, I only have magnanimous dreams of who and what my children will become. You were born a star, born to be great, born to stand out, so don't diminish your glow and become less?

Humility is overrated

"WHAT?" In a loud and somewhat angry tone, I hear you say; but yes, it's a fact that "humility is overrated". In the UK I have often heard the saying "it is not British to blow one's own trumpet or rise above one's station", or "you are becoming too big for your britches". I have often heard these same terms referred to people and even about me in corporate UK. As a "black bright spark" full of energy and drive, you will come up against this literally or subtly.

There is nothing wrong in being proud of what you have achieved or want to achieve without being "boastful" or "big-headed". There is nothing wrong with having a high self-esteem and believing and knowing in you, that you are and will be great. There is no person alive or who is successful who does not have a degree of "self-importance", as Mindy Gibbon puts it in her book. It is a necessary tool on the journey to success, especially as a "black bright spark". I personally would be worried if someone on my team told me that they didn't have a desire to shine, to hit the targets and milestones, and to be seen as a valuable player of the team. Everyone wants this; they want to be noticed and to be seen as valuable and important. That is "self-importance", and there is absolutely nothing wrong with this. There is an old wise saying that "if you don't blow your own horn, someone else will use it as a spittoon". So, blow your horn!

However, this becomes an issue when this need for "self-importance" becomes "arrogance". It's also problematic when you start to see and believe that you are more important than anyone else and start to think and speak of people as 'less than' just so you can be seen as the most important person. Usually, people who behave in this manner have psychological deficiencies stemming from childhood experiences and need special counselling to overcome this behaviour, in my humble opinion. So ensure you balance this:

Be modest, not overly humble, when it comes to your competencies, and never over estimate your competence and your ability to deliver. Further in the book, I will speak about the ability to under-promise and over-perform in order to deliver phenomenal results, which will help you to get that attention you need, and build that respect and value of yourself in your team. Always be authentic when it comes to your competencies because true power comes from being authentic. If you cannot do a task, be the first to put your hand up and ask for help or seek out ways to get it done. This will drive up your value, self-importance, trust and build your capital in the organisation.

Having a bit of "self-importance" and a lot of confidence can propel us to achieve great and important things. In the corporate world, you might be told it is not good to blow your own trumpet; yet, when you interview for a job, you are expected to sell yourself. In other words, blow your own trumpet.

Blowing your own trumpet about what you have achieved and where you want to be is not being egotistical or arrogant, if it's done modestly, respectfully and professionally. Your colleagues expect you to aspire for promotions and for senior roles, and if they don't, then you should be aware, be wary and work with them at arm's length. They will be a negative force and can keep you "in your station" or "drag you down" as they lack ambition and vision. This is not the ideal crowd to be amongst as a "black bright spark". This is baggage and weight that will hold you back, not thrusters that will help to push you up the ladder.

As a child, I have always been told, "The humblest calf drinks the most milk". That has its place and time. In the corporate world of savvy business deals and a cutthroat business environment, if you wait in line patiently for your turn for promotion and success, you will never move; and 20 years later, you will still be in the same spot, wondering why, and blaming everything and everybody. Plant your feet firmly, with confidence, and push steadfastly until you get to the trough or the cow's breast, and DRINK YOUR MILK. In other words you have to know how to play the corporate game and win.

Always anticipate and mitigate against the fact that the milk can become stale, it can run out, or the cow or trough can be moved.

> **Remember, anticipation is the ultimate power of success.**

On your way to drink the milk (up the corporate ladder), you may be told it is not good, not sweet enough, or that it tastes bad; yet, those who say this will continue to drink and become fat, enjoying all the goodness that comes with being at the top. Maintain a tunnel vision focus, distinguish between constructive and destructive statements, and go for it. If it's good enough for them to drink, it is good enough for you. Only you have the power to decide what is right and best for you. Don't forget you are the master of your life and your destiny. You are not just your behaviour; you are the person managing your behaviour.

Don't let anyone limit your potential for greatness

I am really sick and tired of hearing black people, especially in corporate UK, talk about a "glass ceiling" that is preventing them from moving up. Get it in your head; there is no "glass ceiling", and if there is, be prepared to shatter it. Go up with a sledgehammer in hand like a super hero and shatter that so called "glass ceiling" to bits. As a "black bright spark", let nothing or no one hold you back from achieving your greatness. If you believe that you are destined to shine and accomplish great things, go for it. If others perceive this as being arrogant, angry and a chip on your shoulder; so be it. Accept it, and move on. That is only an opinion of you and not fact. The important thing is to deal and treat people the way you would like to be treated, with compassion, respect, integrity and professionalism.

Keep believing and knowing that you are simply the best and that you are destined to achieve super phenomenal results in your career and business, and achieve great prosperity in your life. Believe in yourself and be on fire; set this world ablaze" with your greatness.

In the corporate world, it is important you realise that you will encounter numerous obstacles as a "black bright spark" and that you will need to overcome them to achieve those goals and that vision you have set for yourself. There is a simple technique that I have always used to overcome many obstacles, so they don't become a hindrance to me in achieving my goal:

1 See it for what it is – Know that this obstacle may or may not exist. It can be real or perceived. In either case, accept it as an obstacle.
2 See it better than it is – Look for the positives and identify the limitations and any way around or over these limitations.
3 Make it the way you see it – Spend more time on the positives and build on them. Keep working, chipping away bit by bit on the ways around the obstacle, while always keeping an eye on the limitations.

Most people in large organisations tend to be fearful of the CEO and other senior managers. Why? I don't know. I have never had this fear, but this could be as a result of my upbringing or my political involvement from an early age, working with Prime Ministers, Ministers, and Senators, or the fact I was a senior manager in a global company by the age of twenty-five. I have never been afraid to request a quick 10-minute chat or see them in the corridor and ask them what they are working on and offer my help.

Volunteering your time to work on a project that is from the CEO or other senior manager's desk is a good way of spending more time with the positives, while overcoming and working around obstacles, such as shattering that so called "glass ceiling". No CEO or Senior Executive in his/her right mind will refuse a request for a 10-minute chat from a junior staff, no matter how powerful he/she is. They may have to schedule it months in advance or via telephone, but that's fine, as they are busy people; just be prepared when you get the chance to speak to them and don't waste their valuable time.

I have never been refused a request in all my 20+ years in the corporate world, and I have never refused to give time to a junior colleague either. I find that, especially in corporate UK, as a "black bright spark", they are even more accommodating; so, go for it. Let them know what your aspirations are within the company, and if there are any projects that they are currently working on that you can be of assistance to them. Let them know it's not that you don't have enough work on your desk, but you would like to experience what it's like to work at a different level and learn new things.

Let them know you are more than prepared to put in the extra time and go the extra mile to get whatever the task is done. Also, that you will see it as invaluable, and it will enhance your progress and your growth, professionally and personally. The fact that you are black will be remembered. The fact that you were as bold as to ask for time will be remembered, and the fact that you offered to help will be remembered. When you get the opportunity, even though it may take some time to materialise, don't SCREW it up. Move mountains if you have to work overtime if you have to, but ensure you hit that milestone and deliver what you promised, if not more. Deliver phenomenal results and leave a memorable experience; that is the way to shatter that so called "glass ceiling" and overcome some of the obstacles you will face in the corporate world.

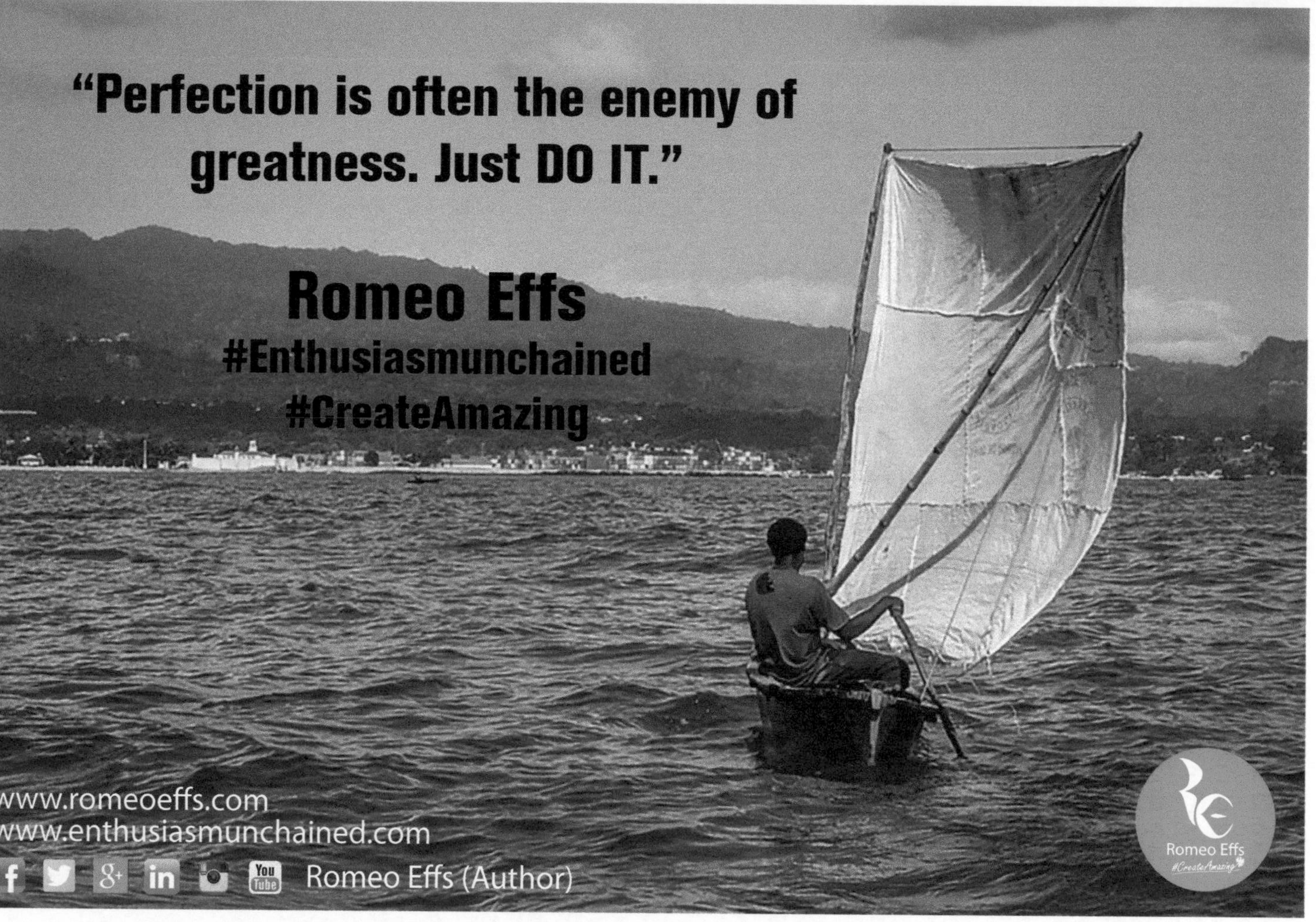
“Perfection is often the enemy of greatness. Just DO IT.”
Romeo Effs
#Enthusiasmunchained
#CreateAmazing
www.romeoeffs.com
www.enthusiasmunchained.com
Romeo Effs (Author)
Romeo Effs
#CreateAmazing

Please Listen & Watch
www.enthusiasmunchained.com/EU5

SIX

Set Realistic IDEAL Goals

"It's not the events of our lives that shape us, but our belief as to what those events mean"

Tony Robbins

There is no one that has achieved any level of success that did not have a vision, and no one will tell you achieving that vision was a miracle that just happened. Getting to their vision did not happen overnight. It happened as a result of setting goals and taking action. They accomplished one thing after another, hitting milestones (goals) along the way until they realised their vision. Most of you reading this can recall the vision you had of having a university degree. You did not just envision it and wake up the next morning, and the degree was delivered in the post; unless, of course, you are one of those who bought your degree online...shame on you! ☺ Jokes aside, you had a vision of going to university, but you needed to achieve a few things and had to hit a few milestones, leading up to this bigger vision of being awarded a degree. Firstly, you had to make it to high school and pass your GCE O-Levels or as they are called today, GCSE with a certain grade. Next, you had to do Sixth Form and pass your A-Levels. You then had to apply, fitting all the criteria, to get accepted to the university of your choice. You had to secure finances. Then, once in university, you had to attend a certain number of lectures, do a certain amount of coursework, assignments and/or practical's, and pass them all over the period of three years. Also, you had to sit final exams and pass with a certain grade. Finally, only then were you awarded the degree. You had to take all these steps and complete each milestone before the realisation of your vision of a university degree.

These steps are objectives that you either set for yourself or that needed to be achieved to get to your vision. Looking back, do you think these were realistic goals and that achieving these goals were necessary? I am sure you will agree that they were and that you enjoyed every minute of it. Achieving the vision of your degree was a logical, sequential step-by-step process. That is how it is with all dreams and visions you want to achieve. There has to be a logical step-by-step approach towards achieving them. Before I get further into this, let me tell you another story for illustration purposes.

The story of the "Dangling Carrot"

I have mentioned the story of the "Dangling Carrot" on a few occasions throughout this book. It's a story about a farmer and a donkey and how he used small wins (goals) to eventually achieve his vision. I use this all the time with the people whom I coach and mentor.

Farmer Joe had a plot of land that he wanted to plant with corn and vegetables by the next full moon...his vision. He would spend hours each day in the field with his donkey ploughing the land, but at the rate the donkey was moving, he realised that to meet harvest deadline he would not have all the land ploughed and ready in time to plant his crops. No matter how hard he yelled at the donkey, it didn't move any faster and it didn't seem as if he was going to get finished in time to plant.

His donkey was a lover of carrots. Farmer Joe had an "eureka" moment and devised a cunning plan to get his donkey moving faster and quicker, so he could hit his daily goal of ploughing a certain number of rows. Farmer Joe tied a carrot on a bamboo pole and strapped it on the back of the donkey, with a carrot dangling from one end in front of the donkey. The donkey, seeing the carrot dangling, wanted to partake so badly that he moved faster and faster, trying to get to the carrot to devour it. As the donkey got closer to the end of his task, the farmer pulled the pole inward, bringing the carrot closer to the donkey's mouth. By the time the donkey got to the end of his task, he was rewarded with a nice tasty carrot. The farmer was so pleased with the donkey's work and accomplishment that at the end of each day he would be awarded with a huge trough of hay mixed with carrots. Farmer Joe was able to hit his milestones (his goals), and eventually realise his vision of a very successful harvest. (I promise no animals were harmed in the making of this story ☺).

Both the farmer and the donkey were winners. The farmer achieved his goal of completing the ploughing of the land, which eventually led to him planting on time. He also realised his vision of a bumper harvest by the full moon.

The donkey also realised his vision. He wanted to eat carrots! He enjoyed carrots and that was his life's vision, to eat carrots all day. He saw the carrot dangling, and his goal was to reach it and devour it. He was focused; he could taste it and feel it. So, he took action, moving with power of purpose and determination. In the end, he enjoyed the reward of the sweet taste of success.

What's your "dangling carrot? You need to set and have these attainable goals along your success journey towards your vision. They are the foundations of your STORY and determine what ACTIONS: you take towards achieving your purpose and vision. (Refer to Chapter 3 for more on RE Success Quadrant – RESQ.)

Set a big vision/dream for yourself, your "Dangling Carrot". Don't worry about whether it is realistic or not. At the start, it is not important.

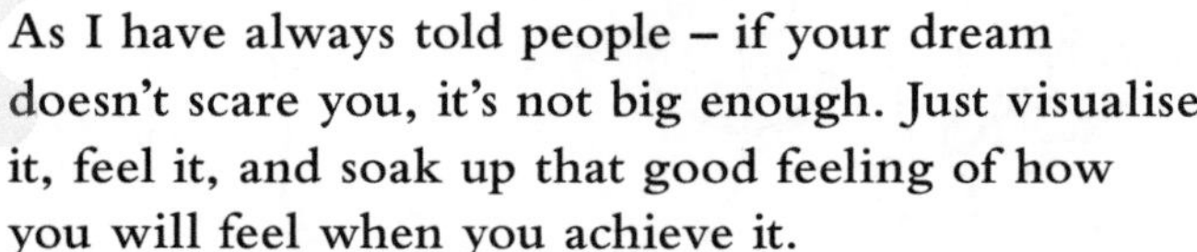

> **As I have always told people – if your dream doesn't scare you, it's not big enough. Just visualise it, feel it, and soak up that good feeling of how you will feel when you achieve it.**

Remember, it is a step-by-step approach to attaining each goal that you will set to achieve the big vision. Some will take longer than others, but remember, success is a journey, not a sprint. It's like Mo Farah running the ten thousand metre races. You run at a certain pace, sprint when it is required to be ahead of the competition, or to catch back up, if you are behind. Otherwise, maintain the momentum, and take each step at a time, ensuring quality over quantity. Success is about gradual, continuous improvements, and change. As my Gran would say, "One, one coco (potato) full basket". That said; push yourself to get to your milestone as quickly as you can. If you set a target to make a certain step in one month, and you see you can do it in fourteen days, DO IT!

Here are some techniques that you will find useful to help you come up with your vision and plan your goals.

Your Story

In this section of the book, I will help you better understand the importance of planning & mapping your success journey, which is "Story" quadrant of the RESQ Methodology.

The Story Board Checklist

It is important when thinking about your vision and goals, and mapping out the STORY Board, that you ensure they are **IDEAL** – Inspiring, Defined, Envisioned, Accomplishable, Long-range.

INSPIRING – Make sure the vision or goal will inspire and motivate you to take action. It has to be aligned to your purpose and be something that you really and truly want to achieve. Make sure it is something you want to do and not something imposed by someone else.

DEFINED – Make sure the vision or goal is clear. Think of it, or write it as if you have already achieved it.

ENVISIONED – Can you visualise the end result? Can you see what it will look, feel and taste like once you have achieved it?

ACCOMPLISHABLE – Do I have all the skills required to go after this vision or goal? If not incorporate the acquisition of the skill(s) that are lacking as part of your plans. Acquire it, or outsource it.

LONG-RANGE – Ask yourself, is this vision or goal the best and highest I can reach? If not, stretch yourself; reach farther and aim higher.

Vision Road Map (VRM)

The Vision Road-Map (VRM) is a tool you can use to help you to realise your purpose and build your vision. The VRM is not to be used on its own, but is part of the RE Success Quadrant (RESQ), mentioned earlier in Chapter 3. The VRM gives you a visual representation and detailed plan of action or map of where you want to be. It forces you to think of a big vision (BE), and examine where you are now – your current state (NOW). It also forces you to admit and record the barriers, real or perceived, that you feel are preventing you from achieving your vision and purpose (OBSTACLE). Write down all the things you think you will need to do in order to achieve your vision. Narrow these into seven key goals. Make sure there are no more than 7, so combine some if you need to. Ensure, as I said before, that each goal is IDEAL. Arrange the goals in chronological order. Set a timeline to achieve each, moving from one to the other and write it between each of the dotted arrows. They then become your seven nodes on the VRM that you need to act on to "bust" through these perceptions and barriers that are blocking your prosperity and success.

Goal Setting Blueprint (GSB)

The Goal Setting Blueprint (GSB) is used alongside the VRM. It is a tool you can use to plan, in more detail, each node of the Vision Road-Map (VRM), so you can take the right steps towards hitting that milestone (node). Each node represents a goal that you need to accomplish on your journey to achieving your vision. When planning each step of the GSB, ensure you keep using the Story Board checklist. For each step, you should keep asking yourself – is this IDEAL?

When using the GSB, it is always recommended to plan from the future to the present. Write the goal on the top step. Think of the goal, and ask yourself what is the immediate task or role you will need to achieve before you can celebrate your goal. Write that on the step below. Then, think about that task, and ask yourself the same question – what task or role will I need to achieve before I can celebrate this achievement. Keep going until you are at the end of the step, which is the task you will start with (E.g. If the goal is to become Certified Financial Analyst (CFA), then the immediate step prior to this is to sit and pass exams. Before you can pass the exams, you must study. Prior to being able to study, you must buy books and pay for exams; and prior to that, find the school, etc.

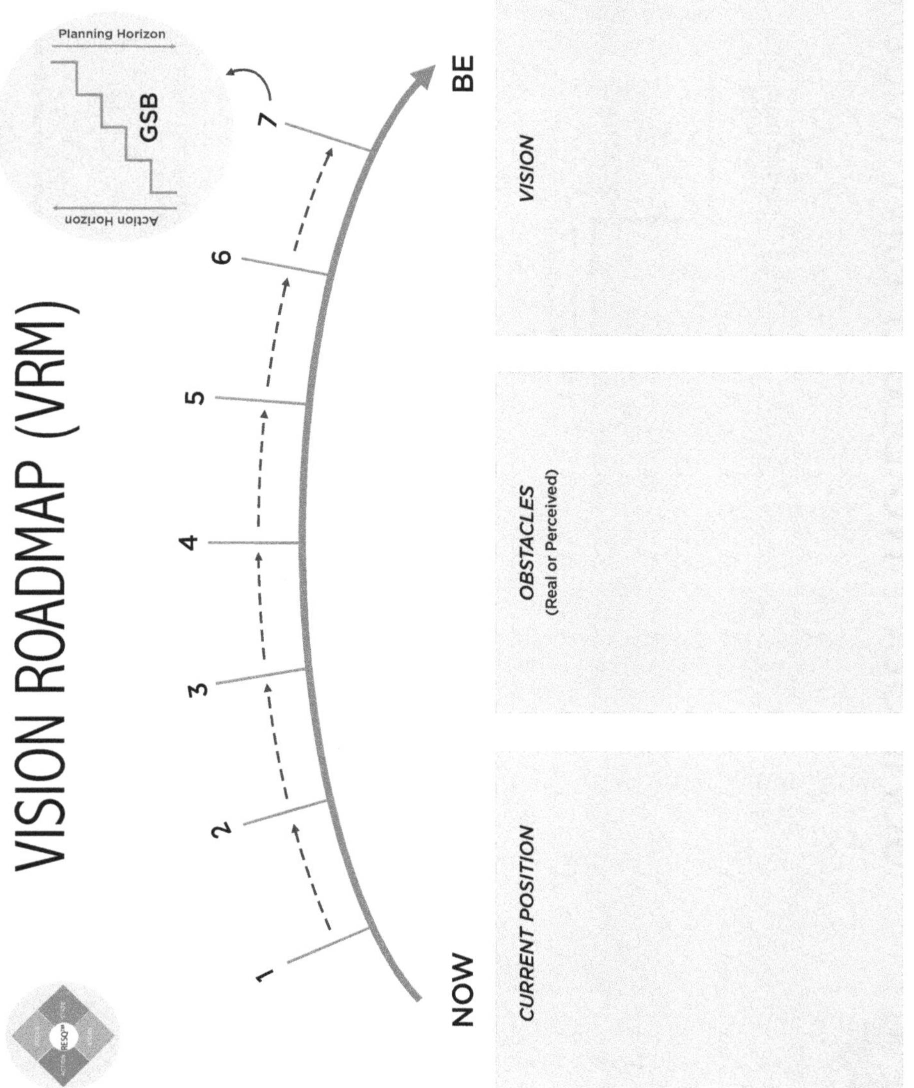

GOAL SETTING BLUEPRINT (GSB)

PLANNING HORIZON

It is always ideal to plan from the future to the present. Think of a goal and ask yourself what is the immediate task/role you will need to achieve before you can achieve your goal.

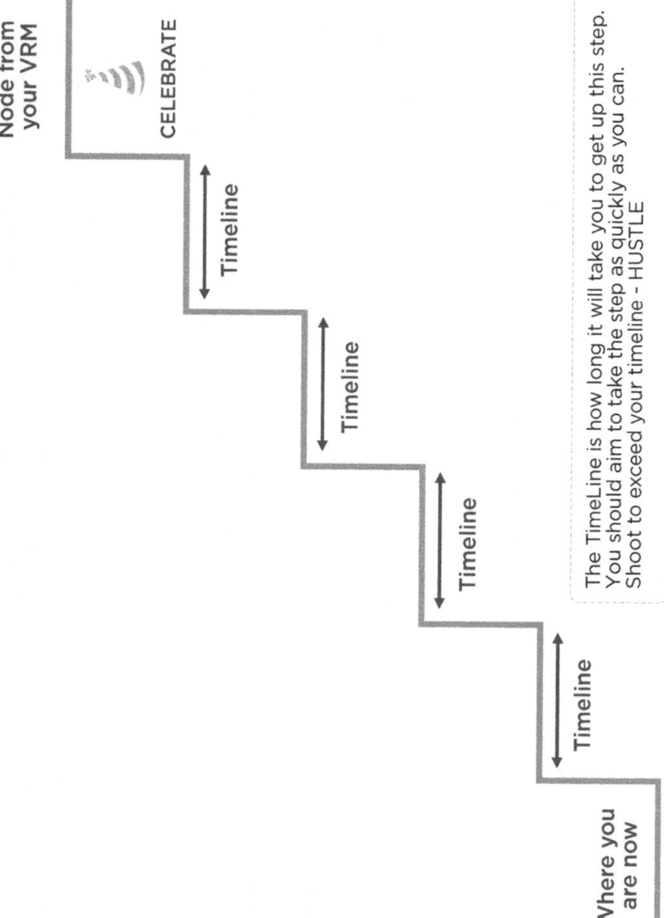

Node from your VRM
CELEBRATE
Timeline
Timeline
Timeline
Timeline
Where you are now
The TimeLine is how long it will take you to get up this step.
You should aim to take the step as quickly as you can.
Shoot to exceed your timeline - HUSTLE

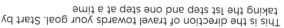

This is the direction of travel towards your goal. Start by taking the 1st step and one step at a time

ACTION HORIZON

HUSTLE

Once you have mapped the journey out on the VRM and GSB don't worry about the big vision. You have already put it out there, so believe it is yours already. Just start taking action. Start with the first node and those small steps, one at a time, until you are at the top of the staircase. Just remember to HUSTLE; move quickly and get there as fast as you can. Once you have completed Node 1, celebrate and then move on to Node 2. Keep going until you have hit all seven and then move the goal post and remap the next vision.

I have been using this methodology for over 20 years. It has been modified and made simpler over the years, but the fundamentals have remained the same:

1 Identify your vision; make it BIG and BOLD. Check to see if it's IDEAL.
2 Look at, and accept your current position.
3 Identify the barriers, perceived or real, that you see are preventing you from envisioning and achieving success
4 Identify the 7 goals you need to take to overcome these barriers and achieve the vision
5 Plan each goal with more precision, using the GSB. Check to see if it's IDEAL.
6 Check to see if the goal is still aligned with your Vision, and check if it's still IDEAL.
7 Take action; start stepping.

After I had achieved my vision of being a supervisor within the timeline I had set, one year of joining the airline industry, I moved the goal even further and set a new goal of being a Senior Manager by the age of twenty-five. I liked the idea of being in charge, having control over budget/P&L, making decisions, and most importantly, helping to develop people. To be honest, I also liked the idea of having my own office. I guess that was my "self-importance" at play, and I have no shame about this ☺. That was one of my "nodes" within my much bigger vision of being the Chairman/CEO of my own business. Achieving this goal was critical to getting to that much bigger vision; as I knew, I would learn some vital skills, get good experience, and training that I would need. Over the years, as I became more mature, my big vision changed, and now I want to own a global conglomerate.

In order for me to become a senior manager within the airline industry, I either had to have a number of years of experience in the industry and/or get specialised qualifications, as the industry was so highly regulated. I was not prepared to work for 5-10 years before realising this goal/mini-vision. I took the necessary steps required in order to ensure I hit this milestone within short order. I found out all the qualifications that I needed to attain, and I signed up for all the courses in quick succession.

Sometimes I had to travel overseas to do it, but I was given the time off, as it was seen as work-related study. Some the company paid for; others I had to find the money to pay for. I ensured at all times that I got the best scores in the class, completing each course at the top of the class. I also found time to help some on the courses that were falling behind or did not quite understand what they had to do, building relationships all the time, without even realising these relationships would become handy on my journey.

I became so qualified that soon I was the only person in the geographic region of a few countries qualified to do certain things, and I had to travel to other stations and countries in the region to sign off certain activities. I began working closely with Senior Managers, the sales teams, and the trainers. I volunteered for projects, went to trade shows, and other events on my days off, building those relationships and soaking up all the industry knowledge that my brain could hold. I jumped at any chance to go work in another department, whether in my local or other overseas stations. Soon I began representing the airline at important functions and on government and other special committees. Most of my other peers saw this as a waste of time, but I knew the importance and what it could possibly deliver.

I was hungry for the knowledge and Know how, and I had a "dangling carrot" which looked so juicy and tasty that I could not wait to devour it. Within two years of doing this, I was headhunted by another airline for a Senior Manager's role with responsibility for four departments with over one hundred staff. The new role came with an office with a view of the runway and the entire operations. I had my carrot; it was sweet, juicy, tasty and delicious. I then set my sight on the next goal, the next "dangling carrot" on my success journey towards my ultimate big vision, that of becoming operations Director.

Career Development Plan (CDP)

The CDP is a tool that has helped me in the latter years of my corporate career. It can help you achieve career specific goals; for instance, if the step between Node 3 and 4 is to move from a Supervisor's role to that of a Manager for example. The CDP is usually used in conjunction with the VRM and the GSB and is specific for where a promotion or role change is part of your big vision.

There are many different types of career development plans in the market so find one that you feel comfortable working with. I have provided a link below to the one that I have used successfully with those who I have mentored and have used it myself in my last corporate role. It was shared with me by one of the most respected and professional persons I have ever worked with and have ever had the privilege to report to (Thanks S.P). The CDP lets you map a route to where you want to be and forces you to identify all the critical components, set objectives with timeframes, and identify the necessary action that will be required. The CDP that I have provided for you to download is simple and easy to complete. It is made of two parts of one page each.

I often ask people I meet in the corporate world or just everyday life if they have a plan of where they want to be or how to get to their vision. They always say yes. When I ask them if it is written or to let me see it, they often look very puzzled and have a quizzical look on their faces. I have often found that the brain retains information better when it is written down. Although I don't know the complete science behind it, I know humans are far more visually oriented. So, it is best to write out your plans. Writing out your plans also gives you the opportunity to share them with people you trust to give you honest constructive feedback. Do this only if you feel comfortable, as some people can be dream vampires, sucking the life out of your dream with their negative and destructive attitude. It is much easier to have a conversation with someone about your development and growth, especially in your career, or a business idea if they can see your thoughts written down on paper or a computer screen.

An effective Career Development Plan must have the essentials of a career map and a personal development plan. In the one that I have made available for you to download, I refer to the career map as "My Route Map". The route map forces you to focus and get into that state of tunnel vision.

> Download sample & blank template at *www.romeoeffs.com/resources*

1 **Where do I want to get to**

This is where you visualise the long-term objective first and then work back to the present. It's the same principle with the Vision Road-Map and the Goal Setting Blueprint. It is much easier to develop the steps/ goals that you need to achieve if you first know what you are striving towards. So identify the long term "dangling carrot" first. Long term here is usually goals that you want to accomplish that may take you in excess of 36 months.

To get to your long term "dangling carrot", however, you need to identify what is it that you would need to accomplish beforehand, to give you an advantage or make it a natural progression, to your long-term goal. In other words, what is the most logical thing to do or step to take? This then becomes your Medium term goal or your medium term dangling carrot. Medium term here is usually something you can accomplish between 12-36 months.

Follow the same process to identify your short term "dangling carrot". In order for you to reach your medium term dangling carrot, you will need to identify what you need to start doing now in the present that will make it easier or make it a natural progression. When I decided to enter the world of management consultancy, my long term dangling carrot was to become a partner. In order to become a partner, I had to become a Senior Executive within my offering area. This became my medium term, dangling carrot. But before you could become a Senior

Career Development Plan: My Route Map

Where do I want to get to	Actions: What do I need to get there			Resources Needed/Who and What can help
	Functional Skills & Knowledge	General Skills & Knowledge	Personal Style & Capabilities (cross ref. with your route map)	
Short-Term:				
Medium-Term:				
Long-Term:				

Climbing Frame 'Journey'

Long Term (36+ Months)				
Mid Term (12-36 Months)				
Short Term (6-12 Months)				

Executive you had to become at least a grade two Senior Manager (SM2). I was one level below a SM2, and based on my status in the organisation and what I was on route to deliver in terms of projects, I knew I would be able to accomplish this within 6-12 months. So this became my short term dangling carrot. I hope you see the logical flow and how it made it quite easy working from the big objective or goal back to the present.

The "where do I want to get to" section of the career development plan is like having a stack of the "Goal Setting Blueprint" one on top of each other, starting with the short term dangling carrot working your way to the medium and then to the long term dangling carrot.

2 Actions: What do I need to do to get there

This is the next section on the "My Route Map". It forces you to identify skills, knowledge set, and capabilities that you will require and may need to acquire in order to reach your juicy dangling carrot, your goal. You will need to identify these for all three (short, medium and long term) separately. This is because they will require different skills and capabilities; you will need to start cultivating and developing some skills that you will require for the long term from the present short term. Look at these as the steps you need to climb to get to your goal.

These are the objectives you need to accomplish. For example, if your long term dangling carrot is to become a Client Account Director, you will need to have client facing and negotiation skills. If you don't already have these, then acquiring them will need to become two of your tasks. These skills take time to develop and they get better the more you practise them. So, if you are currently a Contract Supervisor or Junior Manager, and you have identified that you will require these skills as a Client Account Director, then you should have these as an objective in your short and medium term functional skills and knowledge. Something you can do is to start getting more involved with relationship building within your team. Start listening and offering your help and collaborate with people to get things done. Ask your Line Manager if you can accompany him to meetings with the clients to understand and learn how negotiation is conducted. Read a book on negotiation skills or even take a course. Start honing the long-term skills from as early in the game as possible.

3 **Resources needed: Who and What can help**

This helps you to identify the resources that you will need in order to accomplish your short, medium, and long term objectives and achieve your goal. What help do you require getting you up those steps in your Goal Setting Blueprint. These could be people, (internal or external to your organisation), funding, projects you need to work on, books you need to read or courses you need to take. In the example I gave above, some of the resources you might need to develop your client facing skills would be a wider business network and your line manager as he would be able to get you on some other projects and give you more client facing tasks. Some of the resources you might need to develop your negotiation skills might include taking a course, reading a book or just asking your manager to allow you to sit in on a few negotiation meetings.

The other part of the Career Development Plan deals with your personal development, and I refer to this as "My Personal Development Profile". This sections deals with the fundamentals of you as a person and what personal traits and characteristics you bring or need to bring to the route. Think of it as a pilot flying an airplane. The better the pilot's state, mentally and physically, the higher the likelihood of him taking off and landing at the destination safely. You have already identified your vision, set your goals, planned your objectives, and plotted your critical steps, and now it's time to ensure you are ready mentally and physically for the task at hand of climbing those steps.

There are many ways of looking at and/or after your personal effectiveness within an organisation, in business or in life generally. What is important is that you look after it. Most of you might have never taken time to analyse your strengths and/or weaknesses, identifying those areas of your life that need developing, need growing, or improving. It is critical that you take stock of this and develop a path to build on and improve these traits. Some of you mistakenly think that once you have developed a path for your career, it is one and the same as your personal development. You could not be more wrong!

Have you ever noticed that some managers don't know how to relate to people, or even how to manage effectively? Some are indecisive, bullies, and "brown-nosers". These managers have not taken the time to work on their personal effectiveness: those traits that would make them better leaders and better managers. Your personal development path is just as imperative as your Career Route Map and should run concurrent, and eventually, merge into one vision. It's like driving on a dual carriageway and the two lanes eventually merge into single lane traffic.

Download sample & blank template at *www.romeoeffs.com/resources*

There are some key areas to consider when putting together your Personal Development Profile.

1 **Development Theme/Strengths to Build on** – This is about what you enjoy doing, what you are passionate about in your job; and the personal traits you think you need to work on that are linked to your career goals.
2 **What will success look like** – What do I want this trait to look like in the future, and how will I feel when I have more skills in this area?
3 **Leverage** – How could you use your strengths differently, or which ones can you leverage to benefit this particular development theme? Do you have strengths that are counterproductive to this development theme?
4 **Actions or barriers to overcome** – What are the barriers and limitations? How can I do things differently? Have I examined opportunities outside my role to develop this strength or enhance it? Do I have enough information on how to achieve the "What"?
5 **Timelines and Measuring/Monitoring** – How will you measure your progress and identify quick wins to help motivate you along the way and show yourself and others you are making progress?
6 **Resources needed/Who and what can help** – How will you find the time and the internal support to get this done?

Career Development Plan: My Personal Development Profile

Headline: Strength to build on/ development theme	What will success look like?	Strength to leverage	Actions & Opputunities or Barriers to overcome	Timelines & Measuring/ Monitoring success	Resources Needed/ Who and what can help?

Don't hesitate to download the Career Development Plan or find one of your own and start building your promotion journey. Make a plan, and make it worthwhile to get up that ladder.

> Go to *www.romeoeffs.com* for a free downloadable copy of the CDP and to watch videos related to Growing Steadfast in your Career.

Praise yourself when you achieve a goal

They say self-praise is no recommendation, but it sure feels good. Recognise when you have hit one of your significant milestones and feel good about making it, especially if you hit it within the timeline you set out. Let that feeling of accomplishment resonate through your body. Soak it all in and give yourself a pat on your shoulder. If this is how good it feels to take a small step towards your vision and achieve it, can you imagine how good it will feel when you finally achieve your mission and start tasting that juicy carrot? It will be euphoric.

Cultivate a habit of patting yourself on the shoulder when you have achieved a milestone; it makes you feel good about you. When you feel good about you, it radiates outwards and those around you will see it and feel it. As I said before "Emotion=Motion". When you feel good about you and your state is one of a champion, a conqueror, a doer, you will push yourself even harder to achieve your goals.

Praising yourself is something you can do publicly or not; this is totally up to you. One of the ways I normally praise myself when I hit a milestone is the motion of pulling a truck horn: Fist clenched with hand in a stop sign position, and pulling downward with a loud inward shout of YES! Sometimes, a silent version of the yes comes out, but it usually louder on the inside. This is usually accompanied by a big smile, and then an inward proclamation to myself of "Damn I'm Good" = DIG.

You might think…isn't this overconfidence bordering on arrogance? No! It's getting into that state, that physiology mind-set that you can do and achieve anything you envision. It is silencing that "inner critic" that will always try to question your motives and act as a barrier to prevent you from going for that vision. It only becomes arrogance or conceit when you

start to think that you are better than others or treat people as if they are beneath you. Acknowledge when you have blown through each goal, and praising yourself when you do is healthy and should be encouraged. Start doing it now. Do it each time you hit a target or accomplish a milestone. Praise yourself, and you will see how good it makes you feel. Over time, you will see a boost in your confidence level especially when you tackle a task, especially something new and different.

In the state of self-praise, evaluate and see how well you have done and how you can improve next time. Never settle for the present state; always up your game, changing your state and your emotion, shifting or moving the goal post all the time. It's like one of those energy saving light bulbs; when you first switch it on, the light is usually dull, but it keeps getting brighter and brighter, the longer you leave it switched on. This is how you grow and improve your personal effectiveness; change your state by patting yourself on the shoulder…praise yourself. This enhances your story and propels you to do bigger and better things and achieve greater success. How you feel drives how you behave. How you behave or act determines what you achieve.

Recognise and acknowledge when you and others have shined

One of the biggest issues I have with the corporate world is one of not recognising or acknowledging when you have done something great. I have proven time and time again that recognising and acknowledging people when they have hit a target or achieved a milestone is far more effective than giving a salary increase. It speaks to their self-worth and makes them feel valued. It elevates their emotions and motivates them to do more, delivering phenomenal results.

As a "black bright spark", this is something you will encounter or are already experiencing. Recognise when you have gotten to a milestone and accept it for what it is. Acknowledge those who have contributed to where you have reached. Share your achievement with those close to you, especially your boss and your mentor, but not in a boastful way. As black people, we seem to lack the ability to share what we have done and how we have accomplished it, without it coming across as being boastful. Relay it in a calm and professional manner, sharing all the ups and the downs, barriers and limitations that you had to overcome.

> **Acknowledge those who contributed to your success or achievement of that objective/goal. No man is an island and no one, regardless of what you hear or the media might say, is "self-made".**

We all need other people involved in our story and on our journey if we are to keep on track and achieve that ultimate success. Acknowledge your boss, privately, and also when speaking to others, if he or she contributed even in a minute way. I recalled on each occasion when I won an award (and there were three in two years) for a particular company I worked for, that I would send an email out to all the executive team and all the other employees who participated in the project that made us win the award.

It was recognising and acknowledging that without their input, no matter how minute in the process, the goal of winning the award would not have been possible. Acknowledging and recognising your team and colleagues' contributions is critical in building those relationships and getting buy in for your next project, or taking that next step towards your success.

Reprimand yourself. Yes I Said It.

As much as we all want to admit, we are far from perfect, and we will make errors and slip a few times; it's all part of the success journey. Woody Allen once said, "If you are not failing every now and again, it's a sign you are not doing anything very innovative". If, and when this happens, it is just as important to give yourself a slap on the wrist when you have missed a milestone, or have not accomplished a set goal. When doing this, however, be constructively critical. Do some self-evaluation and take note of what needs improving. Never get dragged down in the pit of "negative thinking". Stay away from the "should have" phrase when doing a reprimand evaluation. "Should have" puts you down and will drastically slow down your momentum. "Should have" keeps you trapped in the past, and as I said before, the past is just for learning and improving on. It is the language of regret; it belittles your effort, your passion and your wisdom. "Should have" invites destructive criticism and allows you to second guess yourself and your ability. "You get what you honour!"

When reprimanding yourself, ask what did I learn, and use words such as "next time" and "going forward" or "in the future". These phrases are better than "should have" because they look ahead to the future rather than the past, and keep you on track and on pace, maintaining the momentum. "Next time" instils hope and boosts confidence for success. These phrases are platform builders for tackling future goals and initiatives. These positive phrases, honours progress, participation, and learning. They build on the future by offering insightful evaluations, constructive criticism, and positive suggestions. So, honour these things to keep moving onwards and upwards!

Get feedback form others, including your manager, team members, colleagues and mentor. Be careful to distinguish between the constructive criticisms and destructive criticisms. As I previously stated before, stay away from using phrases such as "should have", and look out for those who use phrases in the negative, such as "should have". This is an invitation for second-guessing, and opening the gate for destructive criticism.

It is important to learn and cultivate the habit of not staying in this state of reprimand for too long. Get in and out as quickly as you can say "who that". As the great reggae singer Bob Marley would say, "Forward ever and backward never". Simply ask "what worked" and "what didn't work". How do you build on "what worked"? Going forward, how can you do things differently "next time" for what didn't work?

Celebrate your Accomplishments

Now that you have praised yourself, recognised that you have shone like the bright star you are, and acknowledged those who played a role, it's time for you to celebrate. Celebrating helps to cement your state of "DIG" (Damn I'm Good), and keeps you on a plateau of feeling and being an achiever.

I first learned the importance of celebrating when I became a consultant with one of the "big five" management-consulting firms in the world. At the end of each milestone that the project team hit, there was a celebration. The senior executive or project lead would take us out on a special event to celebrate, and thank us for a job well done. I felt so valued, so accomplished, and wanted to push even harder to ensure we did not miss the next milestone. Sometimes, we even got gifts or tickets to events. I started doing this with all my teams and even doing it with my children when they achieved something they set as a goal. I liked the feeling I got when I celebrated these project milestones, and so I started doing it whenever I hit my personal milestones. Treat yourself! It does not have to be anything large or extravagant.

A box of chocolates, a glass or bottle of wine, a ticket to a show or the movies, some quiet time cuddling up on the sofa with someone special, and watching old movies eating vanilla ice cream and Oreo cookies (my favourite...☺). You have earned it. You have put in the hours and the hard work to achieve a milestone, a goal, a significant task, so celebrate and enjoy the feeling and the treat.

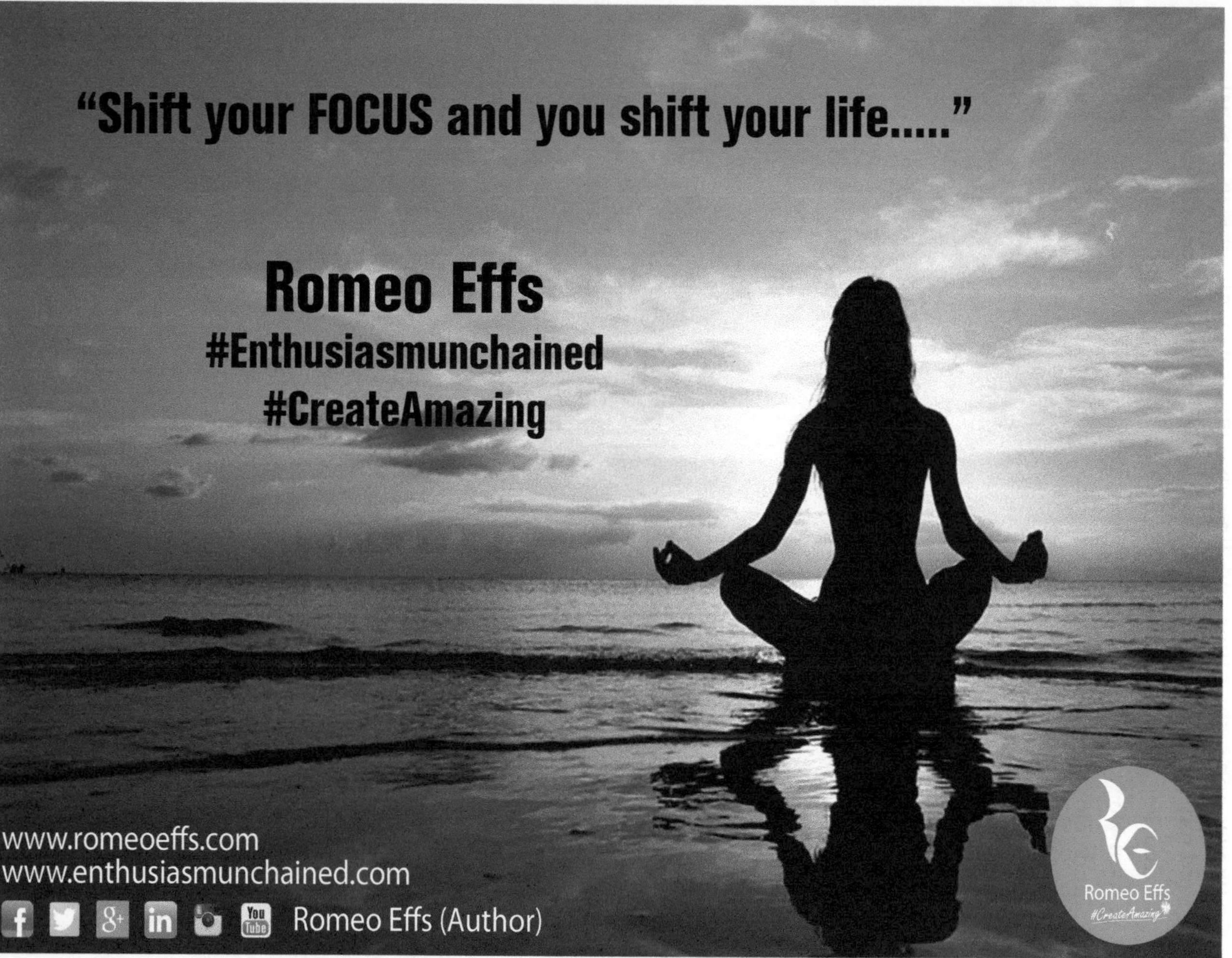

"Shift your FOCUS and you shift your life....."
Romeo Effs
#Enthusiasmunchained
#CreateAmazing
www.romeoeffs.com
www.enthusiasmunchained.com
Romeo Effs (Author)
Romeo Effs
#CreateAmazing

Please Listen & Watch
www.enthusiasmunchained.com/EU6

SEVEN

Action: Become a Subject Matter Expert (SME)

"Heights by great men reached and kept were not obtained by sudden flight but, while their companions slept, they were toiling upward in the night"

Henry Wadsworth Longfellow – Poet and Educator

So, who is a Subject Matter Expert (SME)? There are varying descriptions, but put simply, it is someone who knows a particular subject well enough to have influence in decisions, and discussions, over others. These persons are usually the first to be called or to be asked an opinion about this particular area or subject.

As a "black bright spark", it is critical that you become a subject matter expert in the area of your profession or business or the project you are working on.

You can be a subject matter expert in numerous areas; there is no limit. Most persons find that as they progress up the corporate ladder and towards their vision, they become more knowledgeable, and more of an expert in their field by learning on the job. This could take years, but with the Internet and the plethora of information today, this can be drastically reduced, and you can become an SME much faster. I know many people who have done it, in short order, including myself. Your mission is to be ahead of the ball at all times. Remember earlier I spoke about anticipation as a key ingredient to success. As a "black bright spark", you have to ensure that you become knowledgeable about your areas of business, your task and your project. SME's speak with authority, as they know what they are speaking about.

Get Qualified/Certified

One of the best ways of becoming a SME is to get qualified or certified in your particular field. When you go to the doctor, do you argue with him/her when he prescribes medication or gives you a diagnosis (unless you are my Aunt Jennifer)? No, you take the prescription and get it processed; start taking the medicine, and doing all the other things the doctor rec-

ommended, almost in blind faith. When you become qualified in a field, your confidence to tackle a task in that field gets boosted as you are better able to understand what is to be done, how it is done, and the possible anticipated results.

There are numerous ways you can get qualified or certified in a particular area. There is the traditional route of getting a university degree, which is something I would highly recommend. There are also executive courses being offered by many universities and other institutions, especially in the UK, almost every discipline has a chartered institute of the sorts attached to it, offering short courses for those already in work, or who have an interest in that discipline.

Just explore and ask questions, search the Internet, and you will be amazed on the amount of courses on offer. You can be certified in almost anything these days. My Mom, who is an English teacher, always said to us growing up that the only way out of poverty is education. She told us that the most important thing she could give to us was a good solid education and encouraged us to always keep learning and expanding our mind. She would say, "I don't have no property, nor money to give or leave to you when I die; but if I leave you with a sound education, I will die happy and at peace because that is something you can never lose, and no one can take it away from you". I have lived that mantra all my life and ensured I got qualified and certified in most of the disciplines I have worked in. I have more certificates for courses I have done than walls in my house to hang them on.

Be a sponge; soak up the knowledge

Another great way of getting the knowledge you need to become a subject matter expert is to look internally within your organisation. Most companies nowadays have online training tools and courses that can be accessed anywhere. These online training courses and tools are a great way of building your SME arsenal. Seek them out, and start doing them. Make it part of your story and plan it in as an object, one of the steps in your "Goal Setting Blueprint", or your career development plan.

Speak to your peers and colleagues who you feel are subject matter experts themselves. Ask for their guidance and learn from them. I found this to be extremely valuable, and they were always very helpful. Stop being afraid and thinking that they will not do it or that they will think you are not competent enough. Pretending that you know when you don't know is dangerous for the team, the organisation and especially for you. This could result in missed deadlines, loss of profits etc., and everyone under pressure because you did not deliver. This is the last impression you want to leave as a "black bright spark". If you don't ask, the answer is always, No! So, go ahead and ask, you will be surprised at the answer and you might just save your reputation.

I recall I was appointed Group Project Director in a FTSE company to lead a major strategic project with a big lean towards technology. I was no technology subject matter expert at the time although I knew a lot. I knew how to deliver a project on time and within budget, but lacked loads of technology related knowledge. I was able to overcome this by speaking to my colleagues across the business that knew far more about the technology that we were trying to implement than I did. Some were very helpful, and I stuck much closer to those, as they proved a source pillar, always sending me articles, books, web links and were available on the phone or in person for a chat at any time. Before you knew it, I was offering assistance, giving them advice and guidance because I had soaked up so much knowledge. As a result of all this knowledge I soaked up, I got ideas and was inspired to start my own technology business – TechConiq (*www.techconiq.com*), when I left Corporate in 2013.

Look for projects related to your discipline or areas you want to become an SME in and that are running throughout the organisation and volunteer to be a part of them. When I was in consulting, my area of expertise was supply chain management (I know most of you are wondering what the hell that is, Google it ☺), but I also had an interest in transport technology as more and more clients were asking about this, and it also fit within my area. I spotted a joint venture project that the company I worked for and one of the largest software and ERP companies in the world was working on to develop a Transportation Management Solution. I quickly put my hand up and volunteered to be part of the development team. I worked on the project for 6 months alongside my other projects and gained really valuable knowledge that I have still been able to apply and use today. At the end of the project, I became a subject matter expert and was one of the "go to" persons in the business for answers and solutions on issues related to transport technology.

Keep expanding your knowledge – READ!

Another stereotype of black people is that we don't read. Speak to any marketing expert or advertising agency and ask them how to reach a wide cross section of black people, and they will tell you Radio, TV, YouTube etc. I am yet to see magazines and newspapers in the top list. As "black bright sparks", we cannot afford to be bundled into this stereotype. If you want to be on top of your game and to become that SME, READ, READ, and READ.

There are many books written on numerous topics and disciplines. I am sure you will be able to find many out there in your functional areas or discipline. Seek them out, and read them, or at least read the chapters that relate to your area or task. Get subscriptions to magazines and journals, especially those that are free, and there are many. Not just for subscription sake or to show off that you are getting these at the office and are "in the know", but to read the articles and learn what thought leaders are saying and thinking about your discipline. Who can tell you might be inspired to write a rebuttal to an article you disagree with or to write an article for publication. This helps to build your credibility in the area, and Industry capital among your peers.

Most thought leaders of industries and disciplines have blogs; seek them out, and subscribe to them. They are usually very interesting reads, and I have gotten numerous ideas and "light bulb" moments from reading some of these blogs. Why not start a blog of your own? Just put your thoughts on issues out there. Most blogs are usually what people think or experience. Some people will agree; some will not, but at least you will be known as a contributor to the debate and be seen as having some authority in this area.

It is now more common to hear people ask whether you have "You Tube it", rather than have you "Google it". YouTube is fast becoming the go-to place for information and more and more thought leaders and industry SME's have YouTube videos. These are usually discussions or just talks explaining a discipline. Take some time and search YouTube for some of these videos and view them. You will learn a lot.

> For example, I have a YouTube video on Career Development Plan, and why it is important - *www.romeoeffs.com*

Stop saying you don't have the time. Stop asking where am I going to find the time. Make the time! Commuting to and from work is usually an ideal time that you can use to catch up on your reading. Most of you usually do read on the train or bus, except it's not useful material that will help to advance you and your career or goals. Substitute the free newspaper you normally read for a journal or magazine in your discipline. Start reducing your TV time by one hour per day; leave the Facebook, What's App, Instagram etc., and catch up on a blog or two, and some other articles on the Internet. If you do that at least twice per week, you will be surprised how far ahead of the game you will be and the amount of knowledge you will gain about your industry and your discipline that you will be ahead of your colleagues by leaps and bounds. Remember, as a "black bright spark", you must be ahead and above the rest at all times. So, make that tiny sacrifice.

Network with others in your interest area or discipline

There are numerous associations and groups in your area of interest and discipline. You only have to look on LinkedIn to find out the depth and breadth of these. For every single area of business that you can think of, there is an association or group for it. Most of them are free to join. Find one or two and become a member. Attend the meetings or the online chat sessions, participate and ask questions, no matter how stupid you think the question is. The whole point of questions is to get an answer;

as they say, "questions were made to be asked", so ask them, regardless. You and others will learn something, and usually persons in these groups tend to be less judgmental. At least, that has been my experience. I find persons in these groups and associations are quick to offer help, guidance, and suggestions. I have even had a whole group brainstorm an idea with me, coming up with a brilliant solution that I was able to implement at a company I was working for at the time.

> Seek out thought leaders and subject matter experts in your discipline and have a chat with them over coffee, by telephone, or email.

I find they are usually willing to advise and help. I have rang up a university in the past that was well-known for their expertise in Operational Effectiveness and Business Transformation, and spoke to one of the UK's leading Professors, who was more than happy to meet me over coffee for a chat. We had a good discussion and eventually kept in touch, bouncing ideas off each other. I learnt so much from him although the relationship was mutually beneficial. I eventually went back on a few occasions to be a guest lecturer to undergraduate students.

There are also a myriad of workshops, seminars, talks and conferences held each year within your area of discipline and lots of them are also free. These are sometimes run by consultancies that are looking to share their point of view, or the next best approach to solving issues in the discipline. Sometimes these sessions are organised and put on by suppliers who want to showcase a product or just to have a discussion on where the industry is moving. Seek them out and attend.

You will find that you learn a lot from networking.

When it comes to change, it also plays another vital role, as you will learn later in the book.

Perks of being an SME

Being a subject matter expert comes with responsibility and authority. You become the first port of call within the organisation for any information within the subject area or discipline. Your colleagues see you as an expert and give you kudos and respect, as they know you are good at what you do and know what you are doing. They will trust your judgement and advice.

Being a subject matter expert gives you the perfect hand in the "corporate card game", with the ability to influence decisions and strategies as it relates to that area of the business. In most instances, you will be given the responsibility or be fully involved in shaping the strategy, or writing the policy or procedure for that area of the business.

> **Being a subject matter expert increases your potential for being selected for high profile projects. These are projects that get the attention of senior management and the board.**

As a "black bright spark", these are the projects you need to be aiming to work on within the organisation. But, be prepared; become that subject matter expert and deliver phenomenal results. Getting there is one thing, but staying there and maintaining the momentum of getting the next big project, and then the next big project, will only happen if you deliver those above-expectation results – phenomenal results.

The big plus of being a subject matter expert however is that it increases your chances of delivering phenomenal results as you have far more information and data to use to make decisions, brainstorm, and find solutions to challenges. In other words, you become a "high performer". High performers are usually those in an organisation that get promoted, climb the ladder faster, and in your case as a "black bright spark", shatter that so-called elusive glass ceiling.

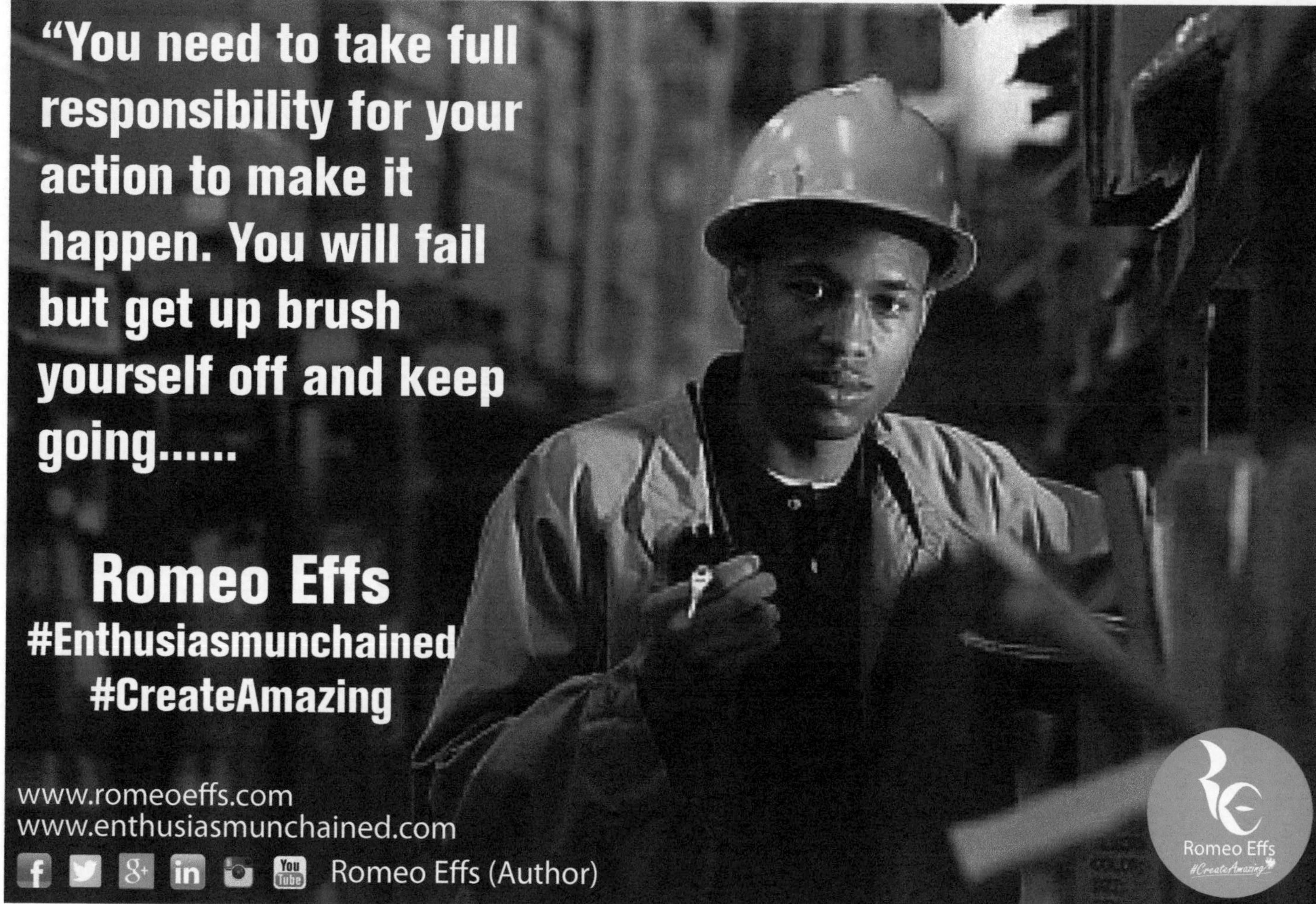
"You need to take full responsibility for your action to make it happen. You will fail but get up brush yourself off and keep going......
Romeo Effs
#Enthusiasmunchained
#CreateAmazing
www.romeoeffs.com
www.enthusiasmunchained.com
Romeo Effs (Author)
Romeo Effs
#CreateAmazing

Please Listen & Watch
www.enthusiasmunchained.com/EU7

EIGHT

ACTION: BECOME A HIGH PERFORMER (BHP)

Perfection is boring and is often the enemy of greatness.

ROMEO EFFS

In the corporate world, results are all that matter, and not love, friendship or being a 'brownnoser". If you are just a good talker and profiler, and you don't deliver results; you will find yourself either out of the organisation, stuck in one place or not having the confidence and trust of your peers/ team. Just know that profilers, talkers, and brownnosers are discovered for what they truly are, sooner or later. Those who deliver results get the big bonuses, and in most cases, promoted. As a "black bright spark", you have to always ensure you deliver not just mere results, but "phenomenal results". That means results that are above target and above expectations. That is what a high performer is.

There are five (5) essentials to Becoming a High Performer (BHP):

1. Know what performance looks like
2. Strategise/Plan/Organise
3. Exceed expectations
4. Don't settle for less
5. Leave memorable experiences

The interconnections and links are illustrated in the high performance framework below.

The measuring and accountability tool to ensure the five essentials are implemented is the BHP Scorecard, an example of which can be found at the end of this chapter, and blank template and sample available to download from www.romeoeffs.com/resources

Know what performance looks like

One of the first things I recommend you do, if you haven't yet already done so, is to ask your manager or team what you are expected to deliver.

1 **Ask and set clear achievable targets with your manager and team** – This could be over the life of a project, over a 6 month period or longer, but I would recommend no longer than 12 months. To borrow a management term, these must be "SSMART" – Stretching, Specific, Measurable, Achievable, Realistic and Time-bound. Pretty straight forward for a "black bright spark" like you. I would also recommend no more than 5-6 high level objectives, not granular day-to-day tasks. When doing this, also agree on the amount of time you will spend working on each objective. This gives you an idea of where to place priority.

2 **Agree with your manager and team how this will be measured** – You can either use a 1-10 scale or grades of A, B, C etc., but ensure all understand this and are in agreement. Depending on who your manager is and the level of confidence and trust you have in him or her, it might be even worthwhile to get this granulated to what percentage of accomplishment will warrant what grade (e.g. at the time of review, if 60% of the task is complete, then that would be a 6 out of 10 or a grade C). It's important that you get this clear, so you will know where to set expectations both for yourself, your line manager and the organisation. This will also give you an idea on how you are performing and which task you might need to focus a bit more on to hit your agreed overall target.

3 **Ask for frequent reviews** – This is of utmost importance, especially in the early stages, so you can get an idea whether or not you are on

HIGH PERFORMANCE FRAMEWORK

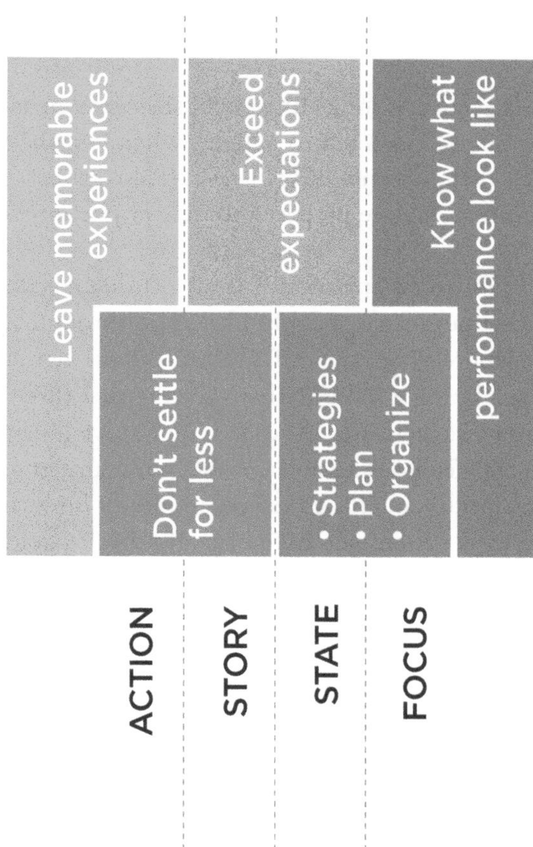

the right track and doing the right things. It also gives you the chance to get feedback from your line manager on your performance. It also gives both you and your manager the chance to reset the targets up or down, depending on current organisational priorities, or your circumstances. Sometimes you might have overestimated your ability to get a task completed, which might result in a delay in the task. Be upfront and honest with your manager about this. Never overestimate your competence, even if you know you can deliver more. Ask for monthly informal reviews or "catch ups" (as they are referred to in the corporate world) to see progress and to realign where required. This is extremely helpful and valuable.

Why is it important to know what success looks like?

Knowing what success looks like establishes upfront what is expected of you, what you are expected to deliver, when you should deliver it, and what will be the outcomes of your task. It also sends a clear signal to the organisation that you are prepared to deliver phenomenal results.

Each time I join an organisation, I always sit down with my manager and agree to "what performance looks like". I go through all the steps as outlined above, and we both sign off. I set time in his/her diary to review this regularly, usually on a monthly basis for the first three months and then every six months, thereafter. At each review, give honest updates on each task, have a 360-feedback session and ask your manager to assign a grade for each of my objectives. This gives you an idea of how you are performing towards the expectations you both have. If I think a grade is not fair, I will push back and let him/her know. Sometimes it's successfully changed, but sometimes there is a rationale for it to remain; so I live with it and push harder to hit the agreed target by the next review. This is important as it maintains and establishes mutual trust and respect. I have always found that I deliver great results using this process, and those in my team whom I have asked to apply this method have always delivered phenomenal results.

Strategise/Plan/Organise

I don't think I need to go into the great details for each of these, as I am sure you have been through this and are doing it. Why else would you be considered a "black bright spark"? If you are not, there are numerous management books, online articles, blogs etc. that will do a much better job at explaining what to do, but I will add some basic facts on each here. These are some of the key elements of becoming a high performer and delivering phenomenal results; so, take the time and explore them further if you need to. These three elements relate more to the actions and support you will require to achieve the objective. I also find using the "Goal Setting Blueprint (GSB)" discussed in Chapter 6 very useful when strategising/planning/organising.

1 **Strategise** – Decide for each objective, what to do, and how to do it. Try brainstorming, or as it is referred to these days, "thought showering" with your team and using "mind maps" to get an idea on what will be required to hit the target. This is not granular, but high-level ideas that you can further develop.
2 **Plan** – Approach each task as a project; start with the end in mind and work backwards, segmenting in manageable, do-able blocks. Always get feedback on your plan of action. The GSB works very well here.
3 **Organise** – Spend time organising your day-to-day task/operation. Do what I call a "TTD – Things to Do" list, and then pick the ones that you see as a priority (I call this my "Hit List") and ensure you get these done during that day. Once I have exhausted my "Hit List", then I look at the other tasks and pick them off one at a time. Having an organised approach to the things you do is essential and far more productive than working ad hoc or "willy-nilly". You can use your app or a diary; whatever floats your boat.

Exceed Expectations

Exceeding expectations is one of my greatest mantras, which I try to live by at all times in every aspect of my life, both personal and business. Remember earlier when I was discussing "Know what performance looks like", I spoke about IDEAL; when setting those objectives with your manager, "Exceed Expectations" is the L – Long or Stretching. In the corporate world, my little secret, which I will now share with you, is to always under promise and over deliver. I do this for two reasons: one, experiences have shown me over the years that there are always unforeseen circumstances. Things can and will go wrong no matter how well you strategise, plan, and organise in the workplace because you are never in total control. It's as my Gran used to say, "Man plans and God wipes out". So, always temper what you promise to deliver. I tend to be "cautiously conservative" (or under promise as some would put it). The main reason being that if the worst happens, you will hit your target and still look good. Secondly, it gives you a chance to "blow the target out of the water", "hit it for six", "a home run", or "demolish it", as you have delivered more than you agreed you would. This is what I am referring to as delivering phenomenal results, exceeding expectations.

Once you have agreed on the target with your team or manager, using the above criteria, set a "self-target". This is a private target that only you know and will be working towards. This is your aim, not the agreed target with your manager. Forget that! Make your self-target the priority target. These "self-targets" can be around the date that was set to accomplish a task. For example, you were given some data analysis to complete for a project. You know you can get it done within 2 weeks. Agree 3 – 4 weeks with your line manager. If he pushes back, never agree to get it done within the time you know you are able to deliver it. Always agree to a longer time frame. Once you have agreed on this, your "self-target" becomes the time you know you will be able to deliver it, which would be the 2 weeks. Ensure you pull out all the stops to get it done within that time line and of the highest quality, so you can exceed expectations and deliver phenomenal results.

One of the areas I am a subject matter expert in is Strategic Sourcing/ Procurement. When you work as a Procurement Director, your performance usually revolves around and, is measured in monetary savings to the bottom-line of the business.

In the initial setting up of my BHP Scorecard, I would never agree on a savings target for a category until I was able to do some analysis and look at the category profile. This gives me an idea, using experience and market research, of the possible savings that I can derive from a sourcing initiative for the product category. This gives me the ability when agreeing a savings target to know what I can deliver when agreeing on a savings target.

I apply the same principles of 'under-promise' and 'over-deliver' for the two reasons I stated earlier. In this instance, however, if the analysis shows that I can possibly hit a savings of Fifty Thousand pounds (£50K), I usually agree to Thirty (£30K) or Thirty-five (£35K) thousand pounds with my manager. Sometimes, managers who are very switched on ("bright sparks" themselves), or who would have read this book and see this secret I am sharing with you, might decide to set an additional target called a stretched target. In this case, I agree to a stretch target of thirty-five or forty, still keeping some under my hat for my self-target, or the "stretch-on-stretch" target as I also call it. I do this so I can still exceed expectation and deliver that phenomenal result.

Exceeding expectations is about pushing yourself beyond boundaries to get the maximum results at all times.

If you can better your "self-target", go for it. Knock yourself out. Then, celebrate when you achieve it; feel good, elevate your state and know you have improved your success journey – your story.

Don't settle for less

Never settle for mediocrity, second best, or a compromise if this means falling below set targets and objectives. There is always a way to achieve that target or objective, so you just need to be resourceful, innovative and creative in getting there. Don't get into the zone of the "illusion of limited resources" (ILR); be resourceful and get to the goal, target, or object. I find that we sometimes give up too easily and lose faith in our abilities to do great things, and deliver the results.

Just keep your focus and repeat affirmations like "if I think it, I can achieve it; I will deliver phenomenal results". In the corporate world, as "black bright sparks", it's the reality that you will encounter limitations, barriers, issues, and challenges that many of your other colleagues will not encounter or have to deal with. That is just the reality; so, deal with it. Accept it and find a way around or over it. Don't let this be a distraction to you because there is always a way out. If you find that you have come up on a well-layered brick wall, reach out, ask for help, and speak to your manager and/or colleagues.

Speak to a mentor, coach, or someone who can give you suggestions or whom you can brainstorm (thought shower) with to come up with a solution. Don't relent! In most instances, when I have come up against these challenges, and I have to raise my hand and ask for assistance to overcome them, it is always forthcoming. Don't be afraid to ask. Most organisations are there to help you succeed and achieve your fullest potential, but you also have to play your part. Remember – if you don't ask, the answer is always, no!

Leave Memorable Experiences (LME)

I remember working in an organisation where one of the business units had a motto that its Managing Director coined – "Creating *memorable experiences* one client at a time". I thought it would be great if I applied that to each project I managed, each objective I had to achieve, and each target that I set. I looked at what I was doing and incorporated ways to ensure I left a memorable experience in all I was expected to deliver. One of the best ways I found to leave a memorable experience is to consistently be good at delivering phenomenal results that exceed expectations. Leaving memorable experiences is about the quality of work you deliver.

Always ensure quality over quantity. Even if you are going to miss your target, or have missed it (God forbid), always ensure that from the onset, you build in the quality component. During your Strategise/Plan/Organise phase, ensure that you allot quality time for each task, you get the best available data to drive your decisions, and that you manage stakeholders' expectations timely and diplomatically to keep the project or task moving at a good pace.

Leaving memorable experiences can be expressed in a number of ways. You could ensure your project delivers something for all stakeholders involved. It could be that you enhance a process creating a more efficient way of "doing things" for your team and the organisation. It could be that you design and implement a program that gives the company public recognition, like winning an award. It could be something as simple as finding the time to have a coffee with a colleague who you see is going through a hard time, to offer suggestions and your help.

Leaving memorable experiences helps you having "raving fans" within the organisation. These are colleagues who will bat for you and your team in the difficult times; and believe me, there will be some, especially as you become more senior in the organisation. You can rely on these "raving fans" for direction, guidance, and support. You can count on them to support and believe in your vision and get on board with it.

Delivering phenomenal results and leaving these memorable experiences will help you to foster and create good working relationships within the organisation. So, do yourself a favour and get yourself on the quality bandwagon and start leaving memorable experiences in all you do.

Henry Ford, the great industrialist, once said, "Quality means doing it right when no one is looking;" this sums up what it means to "leave a memorable experience". Also remember that high performance and quality has or knows no colour.

> Visit *www.romeoeffs.com* to download a copy of the High Performance Framework and the High Performance Scorecard and start plotting your way to becoming a High Performer.

HIGH PERFORMANCE FRAMEWORK

RESQ™ - ACTION QUADRANT HIGH PERFORMANCE SCORECARD

Looking forward: 2H Objectives

Overall Objective	Measurement	Target / Due By	Agreed actions/support
Objective 1 % Work Time - 20%) Grade - % Complete	***This is a description of what is to be accomplished or to be done e.g. the task or responsibility. This should clear and IDEAL***	***This is the due date or the target to be achieved from the Measurement. E.g. Savings of £10K, Reduction in files by 20%***	***Any agreed action to be taken to get support or any support offered to get the task completed. E.g. budget, external consultancy etc.***
Objective 2 % Work Time - Grade - % Complete			
Objective 3 % Work Time - Grade - % Complete			
Objective 4 % Work Time - Grade - % Complete			
Objective 5 % Work Time - Grade - % Complete			

Level to be working at next year: Team Member Team Leader Manager **Senior Manager**/Director

My Feedback/comments

Manager's Feedback/comments

☐Objectives and performance standards have been **met /exceeded/some not met** and a revised personal development plan

Signed (Individual) ____________ Signed (Manager) ____________ Date / /

Download sample and blank template from *www.romeoeffs.com/resources*

"Change is measured by ACHIEVEMENT,
not by words and speeches."
Romeo Effs
#Enthusiasmunchained
#CreateAmazing
Romeo Effs
#CreateAmazing
www.romeoeffs.com
www.enthusiasmunchained.com
Romeo Effs (Author)

Please Listen & Watch
www.enthusiasmunchained.com/EU08

NINE

Think Big, Dream Big, and Achieve Big. You got to T.B.O: (Think it; Believe it; Own it)

"Your thoughts are the most powerful forces in the universe. They allow you to create your own world as you go along"

Romeo Effs

My Mom used to tell me "in whatever you do, aim for the stars, and if you fall, you will fall on cloud 9; but if you aim for the clouds and you fall, you will fall back to the ground". What she was trying to instil from early on was the notion that I should always think big, and that if I did, I could achieve anything and become anybody I wanted to be. People who are great, wealthy and successful get there because they think and dream of wealth, abundance, and success. They thought about it, envisioned it, and believed that they could conquer the barriers and the obstacles; and then, they moved towards achieving this with power of purpose and determination; they took action.

Quantum physicists tell us that the entire universe emerged from thought. Whether you believe it or not, you have the power, an incredible power, to be able to change your life, your circumstances, your status, and your earnings by what you think and envision your life to be. Everything that you know was conceived from someone's thoughts, which manifested in their dream/vision. All the technology that we currently enjoy was someone's thought. The economic system we operate in today was the thinking of Adam Smith who is known as the Father of Economics.

Someone also thought of the modern medicine that we enjoy. These are all big things in our imagination. Some started out small, and others gradually built on them; but the one thing I can tell you is that the inventors or originators all had a BIG dream for their idea.

As a "black bright spark", you have to think big, and dream big in order to achieve and #CreateAmazing things. Just remember that thoughts become things and whatever the mind of man can conceive and believe; you can achieve. You will have seen how many times I use these phrases throughout this book. Not because it's one of my personal mantras, but because it works and has been proven time and time again. Just look around the world to anyone whom you believe to be successful, read their story of achievement, and ninety-nine per cent of the time, it started out with a dream, a vision, or an idea. They dreamed bigger than where they were bigger than their status, or circumstances. They did not know how they were going to do it; they just knew they were going to do it.

Start thinking and dreaming bigger than where you currently are. Picture yourself in that dream and feel the emotions and feelings that come with being in that place. Close your eyes for a minute and just dream of where you would want to be in two, five, ten, or twenty years. See and feel that spacious corner office or that boardroom meeting with your team when you become CEO. See and feel the tailor made Savile Row suit and the luxury car being driven by a chauffeur. See and feel the tremendous joy of travelling the world and turning left towards first class when you board that airplane, instead of right towards economy.

Better yet, see and feel yourself in your own private jet, as I do. See and experience that feeling of being able to easily provide for your family, your children's education or that family vacation. See and absorb that feeling of having an abundance of love and money in your life that you don't have to worry and can be stress-free. See and experience your dream, put yourself in the dream and soak up all that good feeling. Notice how good it feels! When you achieve your dream, the feeling will be one trillion times stronger.

Think it (T) to achieve it

Have you ever wondered why you never stop thinking? You think while you are in the shower, while you are eating, while you are talking, and even in your sleep, which manifests in your nightmares or dreams. You are always thinking. This is because your thoughts are powerful forces. They are the creative forces for everything that you do, and/or become. If thinking is such a powerful creative force, then you can think your way into success. I am not saying that all you need to do is sit there and think, "I am going to be a Manager or CEO", and it is just going to happen. Thinking is the first step, the conception of the idea, the dream, and the vision.

I am sure you often hear people say, "Think positive", and sometimes you might be sceptical and say yeah, yeah, yeah, whatever. Positive thinking works! What you think about and what you imagine configures your mental attitude, your state of mind. This is because your thoughts tell you how you are feeling, and how you are feeling determines your mental attitude and dictates how you will behave towards everything in your life. Your mental attitude determines your state of mind towards your life, and what you want to become or achieve.

Your brain is like an Internet server that never stops running (ok 'tech' people, you might think this is a bad example but, I am sure the not so tech people will get it...☺), and your thoughts are the programmes that let you produce results. What you produce, at what level and at what quality, is down to your mental attitude, which comes down to your thoughts. If you want to change your life, change how you think, which will in turn change your mental attitude.

Thoughts become things! Therefore, you become and achieve what you think about most. You are the master of your universe; you are the master of what you achieve and become in life. Become aware of what you are thinking and make your dominant thoughts about what you want to become and what you want to achieve; have fun with it, think, and dream big. You are the Michelangelo of your own life; the David you are sculpting with your thought is you.

I spoke about The R.E Success Quadrant (RESQ™) with its 4 quadrants: Focus = State = Story = Action in Chapter 6. Thinking is an integral part of the focus quadrant. It brings you into that tunnel vision to imagine where you want to be. When you dream and imagine where you want to be, it gives you a great feeling. It's a feeling that permeates your whole body and soul, of being a champion and of being able to do great things. This is the right mental attitude that you require; this is your State. Your positive state of mind will propel you to write, plan, plot or determine your story and to eventually take the needed Action. As I have said before, Emotion = Motion.

> *So, if you want to become a high achiever and a high performer, you have to first* **THINK IT!** *If you want to produce phenomenal results, you have to* **THINK IT!** *If you want to leave memorable experiences, you have to* **THINK IT!** *If you want to be successful with a life of abundance, happiness, and prosperity, you have to* **THINK IT!**

Believe it (B) to achieve it

I had a dream of doing my Master's degree in the UK and eventually getting my PhD. This image resonated in my mind for a while, among the other big dreams I had as a country boy in Jamaica. Knowing my circumstances, many probably have, and indeed said, you are wasting your time. I did not know exactly at the time how I was going to do it; all I knew is that I was going to do it. I did my research and found the top university in London offering the course in my discipline. I applied, paid the application fees, and got accepted. I knew I would get accepted as a result of my other qualifications and work experience. What I did not know was how the tuition of Eighteen Thousand pounds (£18K) would have been paid or even how I would survive paying for accommodation, food, transport, etc. By the time I was ready to commence school, I had the required deposit of £1500 to pay the university and money for about 3 months of meagre living expenses. I said goodbye to my family and friends and stepped on the airplane to London. I believed that this Masters was already mine, and I put myself in the state of having it and reaping all the benefits of having it. I stepped on that airplane in total "unwavering faith". I just knew I was going to survive, and I knew I was going to make it through the university. The rest, as they say, is history.

I have always heard my Gran say, "Faith as small as a mustard seed moves mountains", (Mathew 17:20) and I have always believed that. Whether you believe it or not, it happens. Believing is the ultimate filter to your decision to make your Story a reality. When you think it, you have to believe that you can achieve it. Believing is part of that mental attitude and that mind-set that's required to act. If you feel good about your dream, and you believe you can do it, it's a double jeopardy to those who think you cannot and will not. You have to know that you can and constantly reinforce and remind yourself that you can. Stop finding all the excuses in the world for not taking action to improve your circumstances. I can hear you saying that you don't have time. I am not that qualified. There is institutional racism. My manager doesn't like me. There is a glass ceiling. I am nobody; I am this, I am that, I can't, I can't, I can't. NO MORE EXCUSES! Yes, you can! Yes, you can! Yes, you can!

Start believing in your abilities and in that power of creation that we all have as human beings. We have our minds, our ability to think, and our capacity to generate powerful life and world changing thoughts and ideas. Kill that SOB of an inner critic that keeps telling you that you can't. There are three ways to kill the inner critic as I mentioned before, but let me elaborate again. (1) Get angry and drive it out, telling it to stop permeating your mind with negative and distracting thoughts and feelings. Kill it, Rebuke it, as those evangelical pastors would say. (2) Be gentle and compassionate; almost loving your inner critic, listening to what it has to say and then you make the overriding positive reinforcing decision. (3) Humour your inner critic: laughing at it as if what it's saying to you is ludicrous and absurd because you are focused, and know exactly what you are about and are doing.

In order to accomplish and achieve the things you are thinking about, you also have to believe in them, and your ability to get there. Get into a high state of knowing and believing that you will achieve your dreams. You will accomplish your goals and you will get to that vision. You can do it; get fired up! Feel and believe that you are empowered and that there is a super abundance of whatever you require to get you there. Use this state to propel you to success, to uplift your life and change your circumstances to whatever you want it to be.

Own it, to achieve it

Once you have thought about what you want, where you want to be, and believe in yourself that you can do it, you then have to take decisive action. Martin Luther King Jr. once said, "Take the first step in faith. You don't have to see the whole staircase. Just take the first step". That is all you need to do. Take the first step and use the tools I have given you in this book in order to take decisive action towards your success. Example – set your vision using the Vision Road-Map (VRM), and plan your goals using the Goal Setting Blueprint (GSB), all you need to do is to take that first step. Do the first thing you said you would do on the GSB. Go on, make a move, and you will be surprised at the outcome and how good you will feel once you have made it up that first step. Owning it is about making that move with confidence and with a feeling of already being there. Owning it is about taking Action!

Think of a car driving in the night. With headlights only shining a few hundred feet ahead of you, you can make it all the way from London to Manchester driving in the dark because you know the next few hundred yards will unfold as you drive along, and it will keep unfolding until you reach your final destination.

When you take that first step, all you need to do is trust and believe that you will make it up the next step, and the next step, and the next step, until you accomplish your goal. If you "Own It", and keep taking one step after the other, your life will keep unfolding. Eventually, you will get you to the destination of whatever it is you truly want, because you thought it, you believed it, and owned it.

Make a decision to own it by taking decisive action to change your life, NOW. You can only change your life by taking action and deciding on what you will no longer tolerate. The secret to change is taking action. You don't have to start big. I once heard a speaker say, "Success by the yard is hard, but success by the inch is a cinch". Change little, but change often. Success is all about gradual continuous progress.

Don't be disenchanted or discouraged if you try to step up the first step and you slip. There is no one who has attained success without failure. Success & failure goes hand in hand. It's part of the circle of life, and you just need to be aware of that and accept it. But your conviction, power of purpose, and determination should be strong enough to get you back on your feet so you can try again. I learnt a very useful nursery rhyme at school about a little train that was not as modern and strong as the other trains and was given a load of cargo to pull from one station to the other. He kept chugging along slowly at first until he built momentum. At some points on the journey, the tracks would go up a few hills, and he rolled back down the hill on the tracks. When this happened, he just kept chugging along slowly, but surely until he eventually made it over the hill. Never give up -"If at first you don't succeed, try, and try, and try again". Never stop pushing. Many of you will want to throw in the towel when the going gets tough, but just think about it, the breakthrough you are dreaming of might just be over the hill, or it might just be the next step you take. Never surrender! Never give in!

The secret to "Own it" are the little wins. As I have always said throughout the book, bite size chunks at a time or as I am sure you have always heard, "one step at a time". Do not hesitate; take that first step towards making that vision and that dream a reality. Start acting now!

In order to be successful you got to TBO

You can start with nothing and out of nothing, and out of no way, a way will be made, if you "Think it, Believe it, and Own it" (TBO). That is how the universe is able to unfold your life with super abundance and success. If we focus on our vision and our story, and believe with almost blind faith each time we take a step (action) towards that vision, that we will get to the top of the stairs. All that's required is you and your ability to "THINK IT", "BELIEVE IT", and "OWN IT"…. Take action. I have had many situations in my life where this has worked, and even though I am still on my journey towards achieving my ultimate vision, I see the goals that I have set become a manifestation of reality, allowing me to deliver phenomenal results and always leave positive memorable experiences.

I had lunch a few days ago with a good friend who owns a few businesses, one being a boutique management consultancy. He started life as an engineer and worked for one of the big five consulting companies, the same one I used to work for, to be exact. He is now a successful entrepreneur, always looking for the next good idea to bring to the world.

We often have discussions on what needs to be done within the ethnic population of the UK to get them fired up and empowered to achieve great things. I told him about my "Think it, Believe it, Own it "(TBO) concept, and he began smiling and nodding. He shared with me that ten years ago he sat down and wrote what he wanted his life to be in ten to fifteen years' time. He wrote it in the present tense as if he had already achieved it.

He misplaced the notebook and forgot about it. He was in the process of moving house and he found it a few days before we had lunch ten years later. When he read what he had written ten years ago about where he wanted his life to be, he was surprised. He is exactly where he wanted to be. He is a successful entrepreneur, and he is now married with children, spending less time working and spending more time with his family. He enjoys doing the things he likes and having financial comfort to take care of his family without worrying.

These are the things he wanted to achieve in ten years. He thought about them, believed in them with unwavering faith and took action; he TBO'ed. All that he had written was in his subconscious because he had written it down. He also had a vision in his head about where he wanted to be and what he wanted to accomplish. This occupied his thoughts and propelled him to act because he believed.

Not everyone thinks this way, and I can just see the expression on some of your faces and hear your thoughts right now, thinking this sounds crazy and bizarre. What you need to know and understand is that anyone who is successful has had to have this kind of mind-set and mental attitude.

I asked many of these persons why they have never shared this kind of mental attitude and thinking with others. They often say people think they are weird and strange when they talk to them about the power of thinking, believing, and owning their vision. This is because, as humans, our society and some social norms wire our brains to believe that things are impossible, that only some will achieve greatness; and that there are barriers, limitations and perceived glass ceilings that prevent us from achieving greatness and #CreateAmazing. Utter rubbish! T.B.O – It works all the time, every time.

I believe the difference between the "impossible" and the "possible" lies within your power of purpose and determination. To me, the word "impossible" is two letters too long.

Since we are not wired to think this way as a "black bright spark" that is destined for greatness, to uplift your life with abundance and change the world, you have to retrain your mind. Make TBO, a new way of life; apply it to everything you do until this new way of thinking becomes part of your mental blueprint. Make that mind-set change to raise your game. All three, T.B. and O, have to work together to change your life into an infinite, prosperous and abundant you. You have what it takes to be that conquering gladiator.

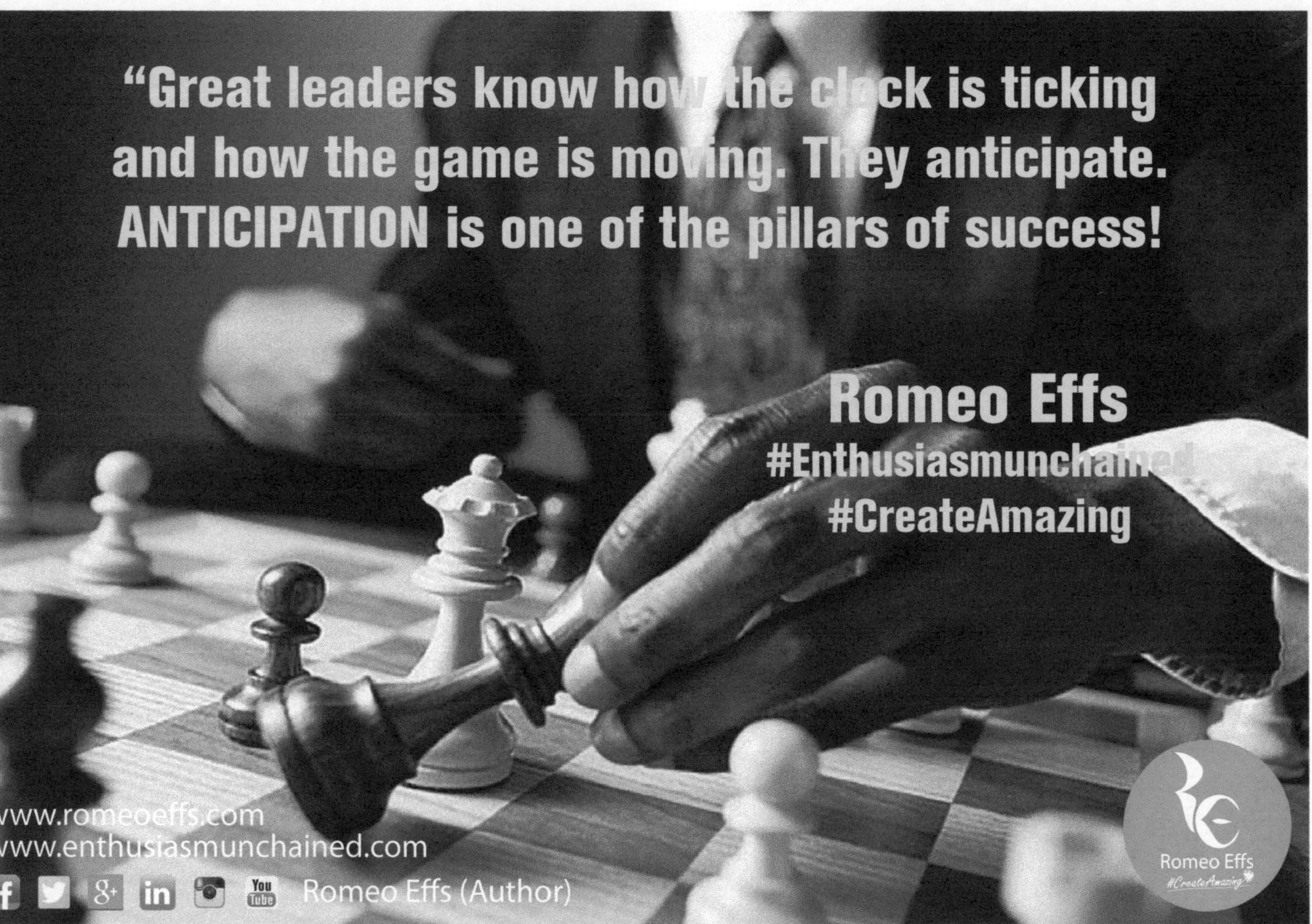
"Great leaders know how the clock is ticking
and how the game is moving. They anticipate.
ANTICIPATION is one of the pillars of success!
Romeo Effs
#Enthusiasmunchained
#CreateAmazing
www.romeoeffs.com
www.enthusiasmunchained.com
Romeo Effs (Author)
Romeo Effs
#CreateAmazing

Please Listen & Watch

www.enthusiasmunchained.com/EU09

TEN

Don't Be Afraid Of Change

"The fear that you let build up in your mind is worse than the situation that actually exists"

Dr. Spencer Johnson
Author of Who Moved My Cheese

One of the most profound books I read as a young Manager was *Who Moved my Cheese* by Spencer Johnson. This, I believe, is the best-written book on dealing with change in life full stop. It's one of my recommended reads to all those I mentor and coach. The story is very simple, but yet very life changing. It revolves around four characters: two rats, Sniff and Scurry, two little people, Hem and Haw, and is set in a maze.

The characters would move around the maze trying to find cheese; this could represent a job, lifestyle or anything you want it to be. They eventually both found some cheese and began making a life around this pile of cheese. The two little people Hem and Haw got so comfortable about their success they became arrogant with a sense of entitlement. They began boasting about their cheese and invited all their friends to visit and would occasionally give them a taste. They never anticipated that anything could possible go wrong, and if it did, they figured they would use their complex human brain to analyse, project and figure it out and make it right again. They "had arrived" and would live happily ever after.

The two rats Sniff and Scurry, on the other hand, would smell the cheese often to see if it was becoming smelly, stale or scarce. They would patrol the storage station to see if the stockpile of cheese was getting low and always had their running shoes around their necks in case they had to move at any time. In their simple brain, they knew that as soon as the cheese started to "go off" or the stockpile dwindled, it was time to move on.

Sniff and Scurry were always prepared for the time to start running through that maze in search of new cheese. The day eventually came when all four turned up at the cheese station, and there was no cheese. The two rats, Sniff and Scurry, looked at each other, nodded, took their running shoes from around their necks, placed them on their feet and set out in the maze without hesitation to find a new stock pile of cheese.

The two little people were amazed that the cheese station was empty and began blaming everybody else for the lack of the cheese, asking, "Who moved my cheese?" They found every excuse in the world to justify what happened, why it was all a conspiracy against them, and that everyone was simply playing 'hate.' They hemmed and hawed and tried to use their complex brain to figure it out and make the cheese come back.

While they were trying to do this, the two rats, Sniff and Scurry, sniffed and scurried throughout the maze, got lost a few times, but eventually found a new, much bigger stock-pile of cheese with variety and taste that was new to them. Even though they settled and set up home around this new pile of cheese, they always had their running shoes close by and every day they would inspect the pile of cheese to see if it was "going off" or dwindling. If it was, they knew they had to sniff and scurry to the next station (opportunity).

I don't think I did the story much justice by condensing it into a few paragraphs, so I would highly recommend that you read the entire book. It's only a few pages and should take you no more than 2-3 hours to read. It's available from the resource section on *www.romeoeffs.com*.

There are many lessons that we can get from such a simple story; the most significant of which is that "it is natural for change to occur whether you expect it or not". Change can happen at anytime and in many forms. Change can be forced upon you by circumstances; for example, a redundancy exercise.

You could be coerced or instructed to change, for instance, by your employer or team leader, to do something different on a project or your work style. You could also be persuaded or instructed to change location or departments. Perhaps it's a promotion or a change in job opportunity of mutual consent, or one that you initiated, such as applying for and taking up a new job in a different company or country. Each of these circumstances of change come with their issues of fear, anxiety and resistance. The biggest reason, however, for why we resist change, is fear.

As a "black bright spark", one of the most important things you have to understand, learn, appreciate and practise is to let go and trust. Let go and trust what lays ahead, even though you don't know exactly what is ahead. You have to TBO – imagine yourself enjoying your new cheese, believe that you will find it and take action; move in a new direction without fear and you will be led to it. Just remember, change can lead to something better.

Change is inevitable

Nothing in life is constant. As we all know, we grow up, we get married (or not), have children, get a job, start a business, grow old and eventually, we die. Things change, and they do so every day, whether you like it or not. Every company goes through constant change in just the same way. This is because they want to survive, grow, remain competitive and thrive. Believe me, change is inevitable. I have gone through numerous periods of change in my life and within the organisations that I have worked in and those that I have started, and I have the scars to prove it. Companies are no longer interested in persons who are going to maintain the status quo. In years past, one of the most significant elements of employment was "loyalty", but that has now changed. I am not saying that companies no longer look for or want employees who are going to be loyal, but they prefer employees who are flexible, agile and adaptable to different circumstances.

Organisations and the way they do business changes frequently. You have to be able to anticipate and adapt, if you are to survive and achieve your vision, whether climbing the corporate ladder, in your personal life or especially, as an entrepreneur. There can be a change in the strategic direction of the business that affects your department, your position and responsibilities. There could be management changes, resulting in you having a new line manager.

This new strategic direction could also result in your position being redundant or the company going bankrupt. Not moving with the tide will lead to frustration, worry and irritability, pushing up your stress levels. Fear of the unexpected is what brings these issues on; get out of your comfort zone and adapt to change soon. The quicker you adapt, the better you will realise what's on the new horizon, giving you a chance to get back on track with your story, that journey towards achieving your vision.

I spoke to you earlier about anticipation, and that it's one of the pillars of success. Anticipation is particularly prudent when it relates to the issue of change. You need to be like the two rats, Sniff and Scurry, and watch what's happening around you; be alert, expect change to happen at any time and look out for it constantly.

"Smell the cheese often so you know when it's getting old". Just like when you are using the Goal Setting Blueprint and you anticipate the possible outcomes and what action will be required, anticipate the possible outcomes for the possible changes you foresee within any organisation you work or your business and decide what possible actions you will need to take if these changes occur.

Look for the small changes, spot them early and adapt; this will help you to deal with the much bigger and more significant changes when they come. When change happens, the quicker you let go and adapt, the sooner you will get back on track towards achieving your goals and vision. Don't let fear be your boss and run or ruin your life. You are the master of your universe and that includes your fear. Fear of change weighs you down and prevents you from moving in a new direction, which will help you find new cheese.

Don't be afraid of change – embrace it!

We resist change because we are afraid. We are afraid because we don't know what to expect, and frankly, most people don't want to deal with anything different. They say that this is the way we have been behaving for years, and it has worked like this for years; so, I don't see why we need to do it differently. That is the attitude of most people when it comes to change, including some of you, if you are honest. Some other excuses that you use to resist change include: – I like it here, I'm comfortable, It's what I know, It's dangerous out there, I'm too old for this, I don't want to make a fool of myself, that's just how it is for black people; or, I am a woman and the cards are stacked against me especially because I am black. Your inner critic, fuelled by your fear, propagates all these. As Spencer Johnson pointed out in the book *Who Moved my Cheese*, some fears are good. Like fear of what will happen if you don't take action and do something is good, but fear that prevents you from doing anything or taking action is devastating.

It is in fact true that sometimes things change, and they are never again the same. Sometimes it's challenging to bring things back together quickly after a change process so that it flows, but it is still better to adapt to the new circumstances and re-adjust.

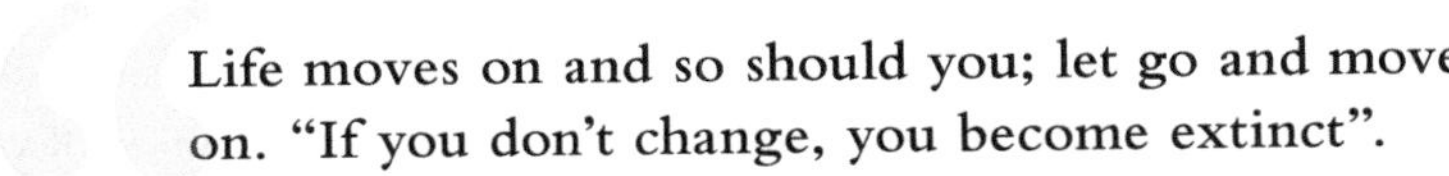

Life moves on and so should you; let go and move on. "If you don't change, you become extinct".

I recall in the height of the 2008 financial crisis that many companies went bankrupt, people lost their jobs, and in my situation, I lost both my job and a lot of money I had invested in a foreign exchange trading scheme.

I was also dealing with the death of my soul mate and best friend in the world, my Grandmother, and dealing with the breakup of a 5 year relationship. I had the responsibility of a family, and other persons depending on me to survive. I had to adapt and do it really quickly, at lightening speed with power of purpose and determination. I had to take a job with a significant pay cut, so I also started a cleaning company, hiring other persons who had lost their jobs, to clean homes and offices, etc. I knew this was a mere detour en-route to my vision, so I embraced it. I did not give up on my dream; I held on and believed in it even more steadfastly.

The detour taught me some extremely valuable lessons, especially about money management. Lessons that have guided and directed other significant decisions I took then and even today.

The success journey is not a 100% smoothly paved road, and no plan is full proof. This means that any story you write for your success journey will have its ups and downs. There will be potholes along the way, accidents that cause you to take a detour to get back on the highway and on track to your dream.

Imagine taking a flight; when you look in the sky, it's bright & clear, pure air and you expect that it should be smooth sailing, but what you cannot see with the naked eye are the air pockets that the aircraft will hit, causing turbulence. What you can do, however, is to anticipate the possibility of turbulence, so you remain seated with your seatbelt fastened, and you learn the safety procedure to perform in case really bad turbulence occurs. Turbulence does not normally occur for the entire flight, and as soon as you hit an air pocket and come out the other side, the flight is once again smooth. This is just how your journey to greatness will be.

The truth is as "black bright sparks", you will encounter numerous pockets of turbulence during your career path, but they only last for a short time if you know how to adapt and embrace change. Use these pockets of turbulence to your advantage, to write another part or chapter of your 'Story', or to write a completely new 'Story'. You have the power of purpose and determination to embrace and deal with anything that will be thrown at you and that will come your way.

Coping with change

Make no bones about it; change can be stressful. It can wear you down and get you depressed, unless you make yourself present and accept the change, deal with it, understand the situation and find resolve. Frankly, as a "black bright spark", you really have no choice but to cope with change. The other alternative is a defeatist attitude that leads to blaming, excuses, frustration, irritation and denial, none of which belong in the containment of a "black bright spark;" no sir, no ma-ham (in southern American accent); it does not. So, since these should not be within your mental state, you will adapt like the chameleon you are. As I said before, when you adapt to change, you take control and steer the ship into its rightful harbour, the harbour of your choice, your purpose, and the estuary of your destiny.

Remember that your biggest resistance to change is "fear". What is fear; being afraid of the unknown. What you need to understand is that the fear you have built up in your mind is far worse than the situation actually is. It's your thoughts and beliefs that are driving your fear. Flip fear on its head, and instead of thinking about all the negatives, and all the things that can go wrong, think of all the things that could go right. All the positive, uplifting things that could come out of the situation. Let these become your primary thought and focus and believe in these. I have a simple little trick I play on my mind whenever I am in these situations. I think of the worst possible outcome for the situation and find a way to deal with it. Once I have found a way of dealing with it, I dismiss all the other negative thoughts and focus on the positives. It will take some practise, but believe me, after a while, it becomes second nature; you soon realise that you aren't afraid to leap or jump into the deep end of the pool, regardless of whether you can swim or not, or whether it is shark infested or not because you already know you can deal with the worst case scenario.

There are two faces of FEAR – Face Everything And Run. This is the face that controls you, holds you back and prevents you from progressing or taking action. Or the one that I like and live by, FEAR – Face Everything And Recover. This is the face that puts you in control ready to soar, looking at the positives. It encourages you to take that leap of faith and just do it. Which one will you choose!

To deal and cope with change, you have to change what you believe. "When you change what you believe, you change what you do". You can believe that a change will harm you and resist it, or believe it will lead to new, bigger and greater things, and embrace it with both arms. It all depends on what you choose to think about and believe. You see, things that happen in your life are a signal from the universe to change direction, strategy, or as a "sling shot", a quantum leap to your dream.

In late 2013, my senior executive role at a FTSE company, (my last corporate job), was made redundant; not because I was not producing or that my team was no longer relevant, but simply put, it was because my new director did not share the same vision I had for the projects I wanted to implement and was tasked to deliver. We did not see eye to eye on anything, and I spent most of my time defending my decisions and those of my team. There were even situations of blatant undermining from him. Finally, he called me to a meeting one morning and advised me that he had restructured the departments in his portfolio and made my position now become irrelevant. This was a "forced changed" which I had to deal with. I had already anticipated this possibility, so when I was called in for the meeting and sat down, the first thing I said to him even before he spoke was "am I being fired". He smiled and said to me, "you are such a seasoned player".

He presented to me the justifications he gave the board for his decision to restructure, and I listened intently. I advised that I would need a bit more time to close off a few projects and to complete a hand-over file on all the projects for the person that would be replacing me. His remark at the end of the meeting was that I surprised him as he had expected one of two reactions from me: one, for me to get angry and challenge his decision and then storm out of the office, slamming the door behind me, or two, that I would break down and cry. REALLY!! That was the last thing I had going through my mind.

What he was not aware of was that I was a master of adapting and dealing with change. The fastest way to change and deal with change is to "laugh at your folly". When I do that, I find I let go quickly and move on, and that was exactly what I was doing in my head. I always smelled the cheese often, and I realised it was going off. I anticipated the possible outcomes once I realised we did not share the same vision, and I knew that restructuring would be one of his tactics in dealing with me. My experience in the corporate world had taught me a lot. I knew immediately how to act and what I needed to accomplish. So, when the change came, I was ready for it, and I was able to assimilate and adapt with no stress, no frustration, and no irritation.

I looked for and found the positives and the things that could go right and those became my primary thoughts. I refocused on my vision and the belief I had in my vision, and came to the conclusion that for the past couple of years, I was off track. Even though I was not ready to move on, as it was a nice, well-compensated and cushy job, I was making someone else's dream and vision become a reality, and not mine.

What you need to know and accept is that change offers new opportunities. When one door shuts, a few more open; you just need to try the locks. I made a conscious decision during this period of change in my life that never again would any job, my position or me be relegated as "redundant". My vision, since I was a child, was to own a global group of companies; I vowed then that I would get back on track to achieving this vision – Power of Purpose and Determination (PPD).

Be an agent of change

I hope that one of the tenets that you see running through this book is the notion that your action as a "black bright spark" influences the stereotypical misnomer of black men and women in the corporate world. Whether you accept this responsibility or not, it's the reality that how you behave and react, and your mental frame of mind at work or in your business, has an impact on the entire black working population in the corporate world. Your responses make it easier or harder for others who will follow you. Think about it! Encourage those you meet and hangout with to do the same. Change your mental attitude and start being an agent of change, which will influence the way you act. This will then help to chip away at the stereotypic misnomer that exists. Enough said!

Companies are looking for people who can challenge the status quo. You have a responsibility to challenge the status quo by being an agent of change in any organisation you are a part of. It does not have to be anything grandiose or complex; I keep it simple stupid. The KISS principle is perfect for things like that.

It has to be radically different, however, to stand out. Look at how you and your team perform your tasks and responsibilities. See if there is any way these tasks can be performed with fewer steps or if there is a simple and more cost effective technology that could be implemented which would make the task more efficient and reduce cost. Pull on your creativity and innovativeness, but don't try to reinvent the wheel here. Sometimes, a simple solution or a simple change for the better is far more effective than a complex time-consuming process. Don't over analyse and complicate things. Remember KISS (Keep It Simple Stupid)!

Get out of your comfort zone; remember, as a "black bright spark", you need to deliver phenomenal results and leave memorable experiences. Adapting to change and being a change stimulant helps you to achieve this. While you are networking within the associations you join and among your peers outside the organisation, listen to how they do things and ask questions. See if how they do things is different and can work for you or your organisation.

Ask people for suggestions, or while you are reading one of your morning articles(and I hope you have started), see if you get any ideas that can make your work life and those of your team easier. Make suggestions to your manager or other relevant colleagues, and get their reactions. You might be surprised that they find your suggestion(s) helpful and implement them.

So, why is change good?

As I have said before, and as the book *Who Moved my Cheese* put it, "change can be difficult, you will get lost now and then, but be confident;

you will eventually find new cheese and all the good things that come with it". There are many new things that come with and from a change; you just need to be prepared to adapt, TBO – THINK IT, BELIEVE IT, OWN IT, and you will find plenty good and uplifting things in any situation.

I believe change is good for many reasons, but I will highlight three:

1. Change offers us a renewal of spirit and drive. It allows us to take a step back and think. Think of a new direction; think of new goals and possibly new dreams. It gives you a chance to renew your belief, state, rewrite or add to your story. *Change is good, and it's good to change!*
2. Change forces us to take action and refocus on the things that are important to us. You are forced to revisit your story, your goal setting blueprint, your mental state and take the required action to adapt to the new situation, enjoying all the good things that come with change. *Change is good, and it's good to change!*
3. Change pushes you closer and closer to your dreams. You have to believe that every situation of change in your life is for the better and is serving you and your purpose. One of my mantras is "In every adversity, there is opportunity". Look for the opportunity that every change circumstance offers, to give you that quantum leap toward your goal, your dream, and your vision. *Change is good, and it's good to change!*

Many people refuse to change, and they pay the price for it. I am sure you know many persons who constantly find excuses and justification for doing the same job until they die. I am sure you know people who constantly tell you of a dream they have or what they wanted to become, but never did anything about it. They become comfortable in their little cocoon and refuse to see that life and the world is fast changing and moving on without them; by the time they realise what has happened, it's too late, and it's harder for them to adjust and catch up. Don't let this be you; As a matter of fact, as a "black bright spark", this definitely should not be you. Smell the cheese often, so you know when it's off; patrol the stock pile often so you know when it's getting low, and be on the ready like Sniff and Scurry, always with your running shoes over your neck to move with, deal with and adapt to the tide of change.

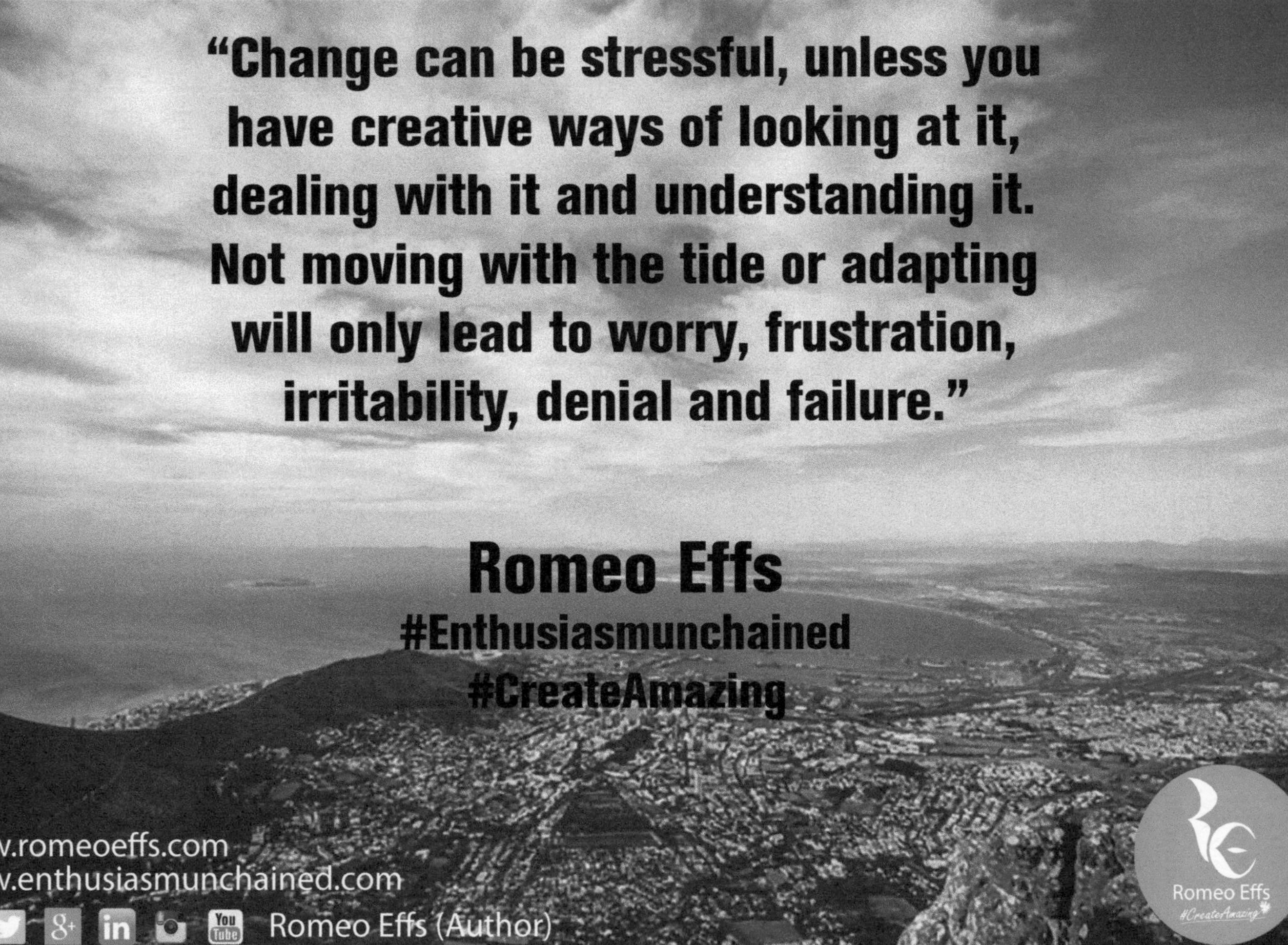
"Change can be stressful, unless you
have creative ways of looking at it,
dealing with it and understanding it.
Not moving with the tide or adapting
will only lead to worry, frustration,
irritability, denial and failure."
Romeo Effs
#Enthusiasmunchained
#CreateAmazing
www.romeoeffs.com
www.enthusiasmunchained.com
Romeo Effs (Author)
Romeo Effs
#CreateAmazing

Please Listen & Watch
www.enthusiasmunchained.com/EU10

ELEVEN

Explore, Maintain, and Develop New Relationships

Treat people the way you would want to be treated. No matter how they treat you, treat them with empathy, professionalism, love and respect.

Romeo Effs

When I speak to some people about the importance of relationships in the corporate world, they tend to remark, "I don't have to like the people I work with; I just need to work with them". When you think about it, you spend a majority of your waking hours in the company of your work colleagues. If there is tension and mistrust, then this results in an unhealthy place to be, wouldn't you think! This sort of environment could lead to chronic health issues as a result of the stress. I cannot say that I have only worked in harmonious corporate environments. Especially as a "black bright spark", you are going to encounter persons who feel threatened by your "bold go-getter" attitude and approach, and the phenomenal results that you deliver. A former manager once told me, "Number one looks after number one". I found it strange to understand at the time, but I soon found out that this is how some persons are in the corporate world. Some persons spend most of their time shuffling the cards trying to win the game to get up the ladder or trying to impress their boss. I am not saying this is a bad thing, but I do believe strongly that in the process of trying to make it, you have to build relationships. You have to trust others, and you have to get help.

The stronger those relationships, then the easier you will find it up the steps of the ladder. And if you happen to slip and fall, as you will do from time to time, then it's these relationships that you have built and nurtured that will be there to give you a helping hand-up again.

Building relationships in the work place is not necessarily about friendship, although that could be the outcome. I have built some really solid friendships with people whom I have worked with over the years. Real lifetime friendships, that even extends to their spouses and children. It's about getting to know and understand your peers, and their getting to know and understand you.

Get to know your team

One of the things I do when I start managing a new team is to have a one on one meeting with each of my direct reports; and in some instances, depending on the size of the team, as many of the other team members as possible. This is usually in an informal setting, usually over lunch or after work over a few drinks. I see this as an important means to get to know them and understand what drives them and makes them excel. I usually do this outside the work environment. Strangely enough, I also tend to do the same thing with those I report to, as I feel it is important to get to know them and understand what makes them tick. By doing this, both parties get a much better understanding of what values they share, and what is important to each other at work and outside of work. I tend to speak to them about family life and before you know it, we start exchanging stories about our children or childhood. We speak about interests such as sports, and even if they are not the sporting type, there is always something that you both can comment on. I tell them about the influence my parents have had on me and what my family was like, and we tend to exchange similar stories about each other's upbringing.

I have similar "catch ups", as they are referred to in the corporate world, with persons who are not even in my team, especially persons who are influencers within the organisation. These influencers are people who can help to make your job easier, who can help to protect you, who will have your back and give you good, accurate information, or advice when required.

I tend to learn a lot from these conversations, and they have saved my skin on numerous occasions. I am not only referring to people in senior management positions, I am also talking about the janitor, the receptionist, the personal or executive assistant, all the way to the CEO. In one of my roles, other senior managers used to call me to get them a meeting room booking, not because it was part of my job or that they were lazy (I should have hoped not... ☺), but because they knew I had a really good relationship with the receptionist team in most of our offices. Whenever I visited, I would take a few minutes to greet them, ask them about their families and how things were going with them at work. Sometimes I would bring them a box of cookies or chocolate. I built up that rapport with a few of them and gave them an open card to call anytime if they ever had any issues that they thought I could help with. This relationship gave me the ability to get the best meeting rooms in the system, at any time, even when others were finding it difficult to find meeting room spaces. Again, this was not because they had the rooms and did not want to give them to anyone else. The system was automated, so this could not happen; but when I told them I needed a meeting room, they would just say "leave it with me Romeo", and before long, they would call or email me with a room confirmation.

They would call around to ensure people were indeed using the rooms they booked and shifted meetings around to get me that slot I wanted. They went the extra mile, not because I am dashingly handsome, and irresistible, but because I got to know some of the receptionists who in turn told their peers that I was genuine, friendly and caring. One of them told me when I told them I was leaving the company, "you are the only Director that takes time out to speak to us and ask us how we are doing; we will miss you".

When I was working in the airline industry, a new acquisition was made. There were several persons jostling for the senior roles in the newly acquired subsidiary, and I was amongst the contenders. One member of the integration team, responsible for choosing the new leadership team for the new subsidiary, was the Vice President of Sales and Marketing. I was in operations and had not dealt much with her. However, I used to have a catch up with her once or twice per year, and every so often, I would send her some feedback on how marketing campaigns were going. I learnt she was vegetarian, and whenever I knew she was travelling, I would ensure a vegetarian meal was ordered for her. Over the years, we developed a good relationship; we would speak about work, and I would ask for advice on career and other matters. So, when this opportunity came, I called to advise her that I was interested. I was qualified, experienced and had the right skills, but sometimes "who you know" can help you make that quantum leap. I was given, not just one department to lead, but four departments to lead through the integration process, eventually getting the role of Operations Director.

Just know and accept that getting to know your team, peers and colleagues' matters.

Talk to people about you

So, this is not about being boastful, but about letting people know you and who you really are. I find people are usually fascinated and interested in knowing about black culture. I am Jamaican, but I love African history, food, culture and people. So, I tend to know more than the average non-African about Africa. I find speaking to people about Jamaica and Africa builds a good rapport, no matter what race they are from. I let them know what it was like growing up in an island culture with a mother who was an English teacher and a father who worked on a US Military base in Guantanamo Bay, and also became a banana farmer. My grandmother had the most influence on my life of anyone I know, and I always make reference to things that she would say in the local Jamaican dialect "patois", and this always stirs up a conversation of interest.

There are many stereotypes of "black people" in the corporate world especially in the UK. It's not necessarily a prejudice; it's just a perception, wrongly or rightly, that they have of the average black person, especially if you live in certain neighbourhoods in the UK.

I find when I speak to people in the corporate world of how I was raised as a child with discipline, and the values my parents and family instilled in me, they seem surprised. What they are not aware of is that "most" black families tend to raise their children with high values and with even stricter discipline than most other cultures. The fact that you are reading this book is testament that you are from a family with such high ideals. The fact that you consider yourself a "black bright spark" demonstrates that you have values to aspire for greatness and phenomenal success.

Letting your peers know what it was like growing up helps to dispel this stereotype and helps to "mash down the lies" that seem to permeate about black people in corporate world. I am not saying that there are no bad eggs, but they are few and far apart, in my opinion and from my experiences.

Invite and introduce them to your culture

During the summer 2012 Olympics in London, a brilliant young lady who started out as a mentee and ended up being a very good friend, went to work with the Jamaican flag draped around her. It was the morning after Jamaica took the top 3 spots (1st, 2nd and 3rd) in the men's 200M. She was bursting with pride as a British woman of Jamaican heritage. She works for one of the world's leading accounting and consulting firms. When she arrived at the office, people started asking her about the flag and its significance, and straight away they made the connection that she had Jamaican heritage. Others in the office took photographs of her draped in the flag. She called the CEO's office and asked if it was possible for her to have a photograph with him and the Jamaican flag, as it was such a significant day for her. He consented, and the photo was circulated on the internal intranet. This sparked an interest in her and her culture. It got loads of other persons in the organisation with the same or similar heritage, to realise that they have something special about them that could get persons interested in them and what they had to say.

My interest in world history and African culture has made me to always seek out events with these sorts of interests. When I find these, I often circulate them amongst my team and sometimes make a team event of it. I am always surprised to see the interest that it generates and the number of persons that sign up to attend. These events vary, from films, art exhibitions, music festivals, and food festivals. In one company I worked, they organised a bake-off to raise money for charity, and the product that sold for the most after a taste test would be declared the winner. I baked a Jamaican Rum cake as my contribution, and it was declared the winner. A photograph of the cake was circulated on the company intranet, and it generated huge interest to the extent that I had to post the recipe on the Intranet. People even emailed me asking about recipes for other Jamaican desserts that they could make.

Don't keep it one-sided, however. Try and find out about your colleagues' culture and way of life as well. Ask them about the types of foods from their culture, and what it tastes like. You might even ask if you could taste it sometime. I often cook and take stuff into work and share with other persons from my team. In one company, a group of us started a "Lunch Club". Each day someone from the club was responsible for taking lunch in for everyone in the club. This could either be cooked or bought. What happened, however, was that people cooked what they knew how to cook best. In most cases, it was some kind of traditional meal from their culture or background. Each person in the club got exposed to meals that they would not have had a chance to eat or taste, otherwise. Each day, people who were not part of the club would gather in the lunch room to see what was on the menu, and the discussions and interests would generate from there. These discussions would spread to the office and even to some of the other offices throughout the UK. Even a board member commented on his blog about the interest of the Lunch Club and the new things he learnt.

I found that these sorts of interactions with your team and colleagues help to bring about better working relationships and foster a more harmonious and collaborative environment. I am sure you will agree that this works in your favour, especially as someone pushing against the tide to make it up the corporate ladder.

What if the people I work with are jerks?

When I speak to those I mentor or coach, generally one of the issues that always arises is "what if my boss or the people I work with are not nice and are unfriendly?" In other words, they are "jerks". If this is *'really'* the case, then you have one of three options:

1. **Live with it** – even though this might be difficult, it's a choice you have. If you figure your time with this team will be short-lived, and it's just a stepping-stone for the short term to get you to that next level, live with it. As long as it will not kill you, or cause you to lose too much focus, bite and grind your teeth and deliver those phenomenal results. Leave those positive memorable experiences and soak up all the knowledge that you can. Learn as much as you can and always keep that "dangling carrot" in sight. As part of living with it, you could try speaking to your jerk boss and/or team about their behaviour and why you find it troubling. Who can tell; you might just be the one to come across to them in a different, but right way, causing them to examine themselves, their work ethics and attitudes. Whatever path you choose, live with it; don't moan about it. See it as a necessary stop on your success journey. We all need one or two of these experiences, and believe me you will learn some valuable lessons.
2. **Change Jobs** – this might not be that easy to accomplish. If you find it totally intolerable to work with your boss and team, then you should try and have a discussion with HR or your internal mentor (if you have one) about a change in departments or reporting manager. I have found that this is more likely to happen if the company is a mid to large company with numerous departments and varied divisions. This makes it easier to reassign persons.

   If this is your choice, then be sure to investigate where you would possibly want to be transferred to and be sure you will be able to work with your new manager and team. I would even suggest you have a quick chat with someone in the team to find out about the team dynamics, and if they are actually looking for anyone new to join the team. Don't burn your bridges behind you. So, ensure that if you get a chance to change jobs, you have a discussion with your former manager giving the reasons why you're leaving. Be candid, respectful, and also thankful for what you have learnt and the experience gained. The other option is to change organisation completely. Explore the possibilities of finding a new job in a new organisation that is more aligned with your values. Do your research because there are many of them out there.

3. **Change your Boss** – This is almost impossible to do unless you have some real clout and power in the organisation. I have seen this happen, but only when the entire team feels the same way and revolts. When this happens, senior management tends to act, or the person sees the effect of their "wicked" ways and changes for the better. Trying to change your boss individually can be "career suicide". So, I would not recommend it. It's one of those battles' that is not worth fighting. Try exploring and acting on one of the other two.

When you think people are jerks and have an attitude, you should first examine your own actions. Ask yourself – Is it I? Ask yourself. 'Could there be the slightest chance that the reason for their attitude towards me is because of my attitude and how I come across towards them'? "Black bright sparks" sometimes have a way of over-estimating their value and strengths, while underplaying their weaknesses. Believe me, I have been there and have learnt a thing or two.

Sometimes, we over promise, miss deadlines, and targets, give excuses and do not take ownership. These could result in loss of trust from your manager and team. Ask others in your team what they think about your performance and attitude to work in the team. Implore them to be honest and candid in their critique. If you think you have been doing any of the things highlighted as negative in your feedback, even slightly, ask for forgiveness and make amends. Correct the situation forthwith and move forward. This is just a "blind spot" that we all go through at times.

Sometimes we push our colleagues too hard and are not willing to offer a helping hand because we think that some tasks are beneath us or too menial for us to perform. If this is the case, you are the jerk. Stop, be silent, grab an oar, and start rowing. You should never feel that any task is too menial for you to carry out as long as it's for the benefit of the team, the organisation, or to deliver those phenomenal results. The task you refuse to do could be the clincher to leaving a memorable experience. As my Gran would say, "The stone that the builders refused will always be the head cornerstone" (actually, I think she got it from Bob Marley or maybe he got it from her… ☺).

Sometimes as "black bright sparks", we tend to behave like Mr. and Mrs. "know it all". We think we know what's best in every situation because we are more qualified, more intelligent and more readily informed than the average person. We "whine" and "moan" if we don't get our way. This can sometimes be very counterproductive and make it seem as though you are not aligned with the team or company's goals and values. If you realise this, grab the bull by the horns and take corrective action immediately. Stop the whining and develop an open mind to receive, acknowledge and learn from every idea and suggestion. Always remember that you are part of a team and even if you don't agree with the team's decision, you must always do your best to ensure the team succeeds. Never let it be said that you were the cause of the failure. This is not good for your career record.

Never let the bad attitude of your manager or team be an excuse for poor performance. Never let it affect or reflect on your performance. Frank Sinatra once said, "Success is the sweetest revenge".

If your manager and/or colleagues are idiots and playing the ass, keep on out-performing, delivering those phenomenal results, and leaving those positive memorable experiences. Continue delivering high performance, giving credit where credit is due, and doing your best for your boss and your team. Pulling or scaling back, will only hurt you, and will have an impact on the timelines and possible outcomes of your goals, dreams and aspirations. Remember, your vested interest in all this is to attain that promotion, get that exposure or gain experience to propel you towards that ultimate purpose and vision.

Surround yourself with people who are going to lift you up and thrust you higher

Having worked in the aviation industry for a number of years, I know that a pilot is usually worried about four things when he is about to take off or land – drag, weight, lift and thrust. If there is too much drag and weight, it makes it harder for the aircraft to take off, as the plane will find it more difficult to get to the speed it needs, so it can lift off and thrust forward. The same applies to your success journey. Surround yourself with people who are either lifters and/or thrusters.

Success follows success. If you surround yourself with people who are just as driven and as ambitious as you are, you will find that your success journey becomes easier as they will be able to advise and share ideas that will be of help. This could be one or more person, internal to your organisation or external that you can call upon for some guidance and direction when you are stuck. I have had a few of these; some have even been former managers. These are not necessarily mentors, but are more like friends or associates who share the same values and drive to be as phenomenally successful as you are in their particular field. I have met some real superstars over the life of my young career, from all ages and backgrounds that are as driven and as hungry to achieve greatness as I am. With some, I have started and ran successful businesses, and become friends; and others, we catch-up once in a while. But what keeps us on the same planet is the fact that we share similar ideals. One such individual is Ingrid Riley – Founder & CEO of GetConnected and Founder & Executive Director of Connectimass Foundation, and the Tech Guru of the Caribbean. Ingrid and I have known each other since high school. We have sat on many company boards together, and started numerous organisations and businesses; but no matter where we are in the world, we always make it a point of our duty to connect as often as possible and to give each other a serious kick up the backside to propel us to accomplish more and achieve even greater things. We encourage each other, constantly bounce ideas off each other, and at times, act as an accountability buddy. People think we are over achievers because we are never satisfied with where we are and are constantly pushing the boundaries to get to that next level. That is what we do as "black bright sparks". It's part of our nature as it is part of yours. Find that person or persons that can become your accountability buddy and push each other to achieve greatness. As Les Brown, one of the people who has inspired me would say, "If you find out you are the brightest person in your group, you need to find a new group. You need to examine whom you surround yourself with and upgrade your relationships".

Success leaves a trail of breadcrumbs. Seek out and find a valuable mentor, coach and/or sponsor. Not every mentor or coach will add value to your career progression or success journey. Some of them, especially those "appointed" internally, are never as useful. The internal ones that I find more valuable are those that you ask, and they consent. I found external mentors far more objective and open. They tend to look at and help you more with your holistic development. You should be comfortable with your mentor, and it should not matter what race they are from. It does not mean that because you are black or an ethnic minority, you need to get a mentor from the same race.

The best mentor I have had in my career thus far is my current mentor, who happens to be a white English female (used for emphasis). She has worked in a multi-cultured organisation at a senior executive level and has worked in numerous countries throughout the world with one of the largest financial institutions in the world. She also sits on numerous boards of private companies and public bodies. She took time to understand my culture and upbringing, and how I think and tick.

She guides and advises me on my career, my personal life and surprisingly, at one of our meetings, she started asking me about how my finances were structured. I was very pleased because this was an area I was struggling in and needed some help with, but was afraid to discuss with her even though we had a really good rapport. She was well prepared and was able to give me names and contact details of persons I could speak to who would give me the right professional financial advice. I am happy to say that today I have a sound financial plan that is going well. At one meeting when there were issues brewing between my CEO and I, she was able to give impartial and candid advice of what she saw as the issue and what I needed to do about it. When she saw that it was time for me to start looking for a new role externally, as I was not progressing in the right direction and not having the right tasks and experiences, she told me so and advised how to go about it. She had walked a similar trail that I was walking, so she knew the possible pitfalls and dips that I would or could experience. She steered me away from some of the pitfalls and in some cases over them. I am so inspired by her and what she has achieved in her life, and even more so, the impact that she has had on my life and my success journey. I have learnt a lot of information and valuable lessons from her, and I have put it in practice with those I mentor.

As a "black bright sparks", you need a mentor or coach, someone who wants to see you achieve greatness and #CreateAmazing. This could even be someone with whom you have a paid arrangement. As long as this person is passionate about your success and guides you along, it's worth it. If you don't already have an internal mentor within your organisation and an external mentor to develop you holistically, I strongly suggest you find one. Start looking and asking around now, or feel free to contact us using the link below.

> We offer a wide array of mentoring and coaching programs, so see *www.romeoeffs.com* for details.

An internal sponsor is also essential. A good internal sponsor is invaluable and will help you achieve your career dream much quicker. This should be someone senior in the organisation, preferably with some influence. Sponsors are most useful to open doors within the organisation for you, helping you to get that next internal opportunity. They become your advocate in the organisation and will support and "bat" for you once they believe in you. So, find a sponsor that believes in you. The problem I find with most "black bright sparks" is that we tend to be "over-mentored" and "under-sponsored". Mentors and sponsors work hand in hand; but if you have to choose, I would strongly suggest you choose an internal sponsor rather than an internal mentor.

Be authentic and genuine

The most important facet you can have in exploring, maintaining and developing new relationships is to "be honest, authentic and genuine". Being authentic is an expression of who you really are as a person. It is a reflection of what you are feeling, thinking, and believing inside. Are you truthful with, what you say and how you say it? Are you presenting the facts, or just mere instinctive, hearsay or gut feeling? If it is any of these, are you making it clear that it is so, and not the fact? Being genuine is how you relate to others. Are you warm and caring? Do you display a friendly disposition? People can sniff out disingenuous people a mile away. When you deal with people honestly and up front, they respect you more and will be more willing to offer their help. Remember as a "black bright spark", you already have to contend with the perceptions and stereotypes disadvantages, and how you are seen at face value. Adding to that, being fake and dishonest will only add fuel to the fire and cement the stereotype further.

Let people know your true self, your real values, and true purpose.

Don't be afraid to let them know what your dreams and visions are, and how you plan to achieve them. Let them know that in your belly, your spine, your feet, your hands, and your brain that you have a burning desire to succeed and achieve greatness. Let them know that you are willing to push hard and fast to get to where you want to be. When you speak to them with regard to your upbringing, tell the truth. Don't be afraid of where you were born, grew up, live or have lived. Be proud of where you have come from and what you have achieved, and be even more proud of where you will be. It does not matter if you came from the ghetto, or slums with very poor upbringing with parents that could barely afford to feed you or send you to school.

Do not be afraid to let them know that you are from a lower middle class family with a single Mom who was a teacher or cleaner, who struggled to make ends meet, but still ensured you had the best education, food to eat and clothes on your back by doing two or three other jobs, besides her teaching or cleaning. Don't be afraid either to also say, if you are from an upper middle class or wealthy family who could afford to send you to the best schools, you travelled regularly, or you did not want for anything growing up. No matter what your circumstances, be proud of it and never allow anyone to make you feel belittled or inferior because of it.

You had no control over your circumstances as a child of how you grew up; so, don't let it be a burden. Shake that off, put down that baggage, or better yet, put it in a rocket and launch it into space. That's excess baggage you don't need to have. It will weigh and drag you down on your success journey. You have no control over the past, and that is also one thing you cannot change or control. What you have control over is your future, how it is shaped and what it turns out to be like. Take control of your future and become the driver and master.

I was once mentoring a guy, who was living and working in London. When I started mentoring him, he told me he was the manager of a restaurant and a small guesthouse. We met a couple of times, and he would tell me stories of his upbringing, of the struggles he went through as a child, and how he came to be in the UK.

As I usually do, I would invite some of the persons I mentor to some of the events I attend to give them exposure and widen their horizons. I invited that young man to a few of these events, but noticed he would always have a different version of his life story or the experiences in his life. He also always wanted to be the centre of attraction at the events, so he would speak much louder and always have some elaborate stories to tell about Africa. I confronted him during one of our one to one sessions about some of the things he had said.

He acknowledged that some were exaggerated, but that he meant no harm. What he did not realise was that others at the event realised that some of what he said was over the top, and in some cases, downright lies, based on their experiences and knowledge. They immediately discounted him and saw him as disingenuous and also untrustworthy. If there was someone in that room that could have been of any assistance to him, that opportunity was blown away because of his behaviour. His dream of being the General Manager for a 5-Star hotel could have been slowed or destroyed because of such dastardly acts of not being genuine and honest. You never know who will be listening or whom you will meet. If they are like me, with a good memory, then they might just recall what you said to them years ago and compare it to what you will say to them in the present. If you were genuine and honest then, it is more likely that you will say the same thing now because it is the truth. It is much easier to remember something that actually happened than something fabricated.

When speaking to people at work or as a mentor, be sure you are comfortable with them and choose to share certain things only with those you are comfortable with.

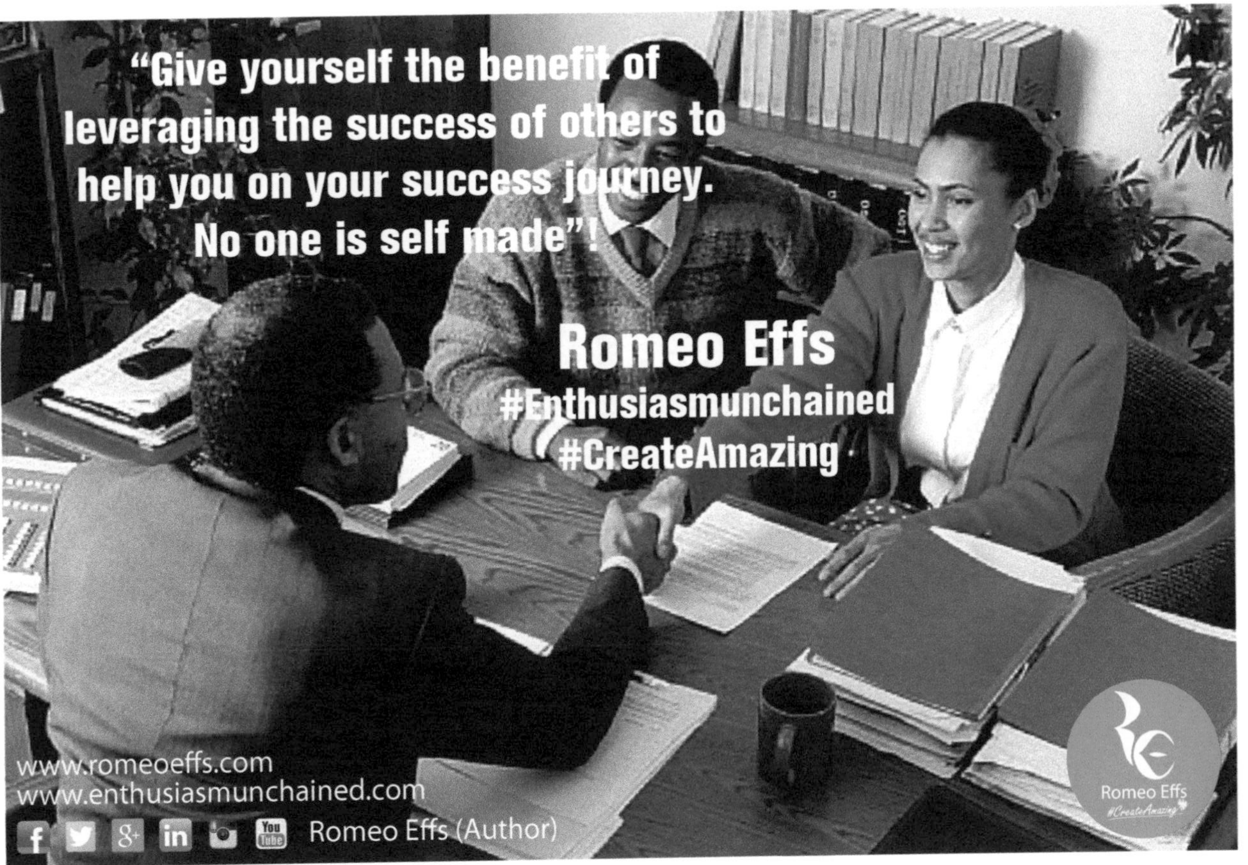
"Give yourself the benefit of
leveraging the success of others to
help you on your success journey.
No one is self made"!
Romeo Effs
#Enthusiasmunchained
#CreateAmazing
www.romeoeffs.com
www.enthusiasmunchained.com
Romeo Effs (Author)
Romeo Effs

Please Listen & Watch
www.enthusiasmunchained.com/EU11

TWELVE

Give Back and Help Dispel the Perceived Stereotype

Success is not about how much money you make; it's about the difference you make in people's lives.

Michelle Obama
First Lady of the United States of America

One thing that has always astonished me about black people that I have met, in corporate UK in particular, is a sense of fear of relating and speaking openly to other black people in the office, especially if you are more senior to them.

What the hell is this all about? I once asked a colleague from another company if a group of us could use a meeting room in his office after working hours to discuss the plans we had for a community project we were trying to implement. He was also part of the core group planning this project. The core group was made up of six black people, all professionals in really high profile jobs. He was hesitant and fearful remarking, "What do you think people would say seeing a bunch of black people entering the office after work hours? Plus, what if something should go missing from the office, they will all want to blame us for it". Although this thought in people's head might be true, WHO CARES!

This is a result of a mind-set that has been embedded with self-perception and beliefs of what others think and feel about you as a black person. Get over it! The only thing that is important is how you feel and think about yourself. Your perception of who you are and what you will become is going to be your springboard to #CreateAmazing and greatness. This is far more important than what others perceive of you. This kind of mind-set, I believe, is the stumbling block to us reaching out more to give a helping hand to our fellow brothers and sisters of colour. I am not saying that we should only help our black sisters and brothers, but we should make an effort to reach out to them more. In all the organisations that I have worked in, I have made if a part of my duty to seek out and reach out to other "black bright sparks" in the organisation. Not because I want to be nice, or friendly, but because usually I am the only black face at the senior level within that organisation and, instinctively, I am inspired to help someone else reach that level. We are greater than the sum of our own ambitions, and if we each help one, it will multiply and snowball from one to one, and then to many.

Mentoring

I have been mentoring ever since I started work life. I had no choice as I was one of a very few from my district in St. Mary, Jamaica, to make it to university and to work in a good job. I was also running a successful event management company doing some of the largest events in Jamaica, heavily involved in politics, an executive member of several national voluntary organisations and clubs, such as Rotary and Jaycees, and sat on a number of company boards. I have been interviewed on television, radio, and newspapers, and even had feature spreads in international magazines. At a young age, I was pushing all boundaries, and I was heading towards conquering the world. So, I was always being asked how I have been able to accomplish so much at such a young age. Especially when someone younger or even in my age group asked me this question, I always felt inspired, with a desire to show and give them tips and ideas of what to do to achieve the success they wanted for themselves. I would even open up new opportunities for them, like calling in a favour to get them a job, or into a school with reduced fees etc., or arrange for them to meet someone who had more experience in their chosen field, so they could get the right guidance they required.

Over the years, I have helped mentor countless individuals, and they have made me proud of what they have achieved. I remember when I was an Airports and Cargo Development Manager, I spotted a young man with great potential who was employed as a ramp attendant (baggage loader). His work ethic, diction, and attention to detail were far greater than any of the other guys on the ramp (airside where the aircraft parks). He was constantly asking questions about other areas of the industry.

I noticed he would prefer to work on the passenger side, helping the Check In Agents remove the bags from the scale and load them on the conveyor belt, (these were the days before airports were fully automated as you can see.... ☺), and assisting passengers in completing the correct forms, etc. I decided that this young man was not cut out to be a baggage loader, and he was in fact a "black bright spark" who just needed some guidance and mentoring.

I started showing and teaching him a few of the procedures and gave him some of the manuals to read. Even though he was not certified to do most of what I taught or showed him, I believed in the power of knowledge, and I believed in him and his dream to become an Agent. That was his dream, to become an Airline Operations Agent. Even though I knew he could achieve greater, that is what success looked like to him, and that was going to be my starting point, so as not to scare him with too much too soon.

A quantum leap came for him when I was launching a new small package service for the airline and needed to train a few agents on the new procedures. I included him in the training sessions, and he excelled, much to the surprise of the tutors. He was given the task of handling the small packages counter, alongside his responsibility of baggage handling. Gradually, as the service picked up, this became his full time job. Today, he is a Senior Manager in the Airline industry. This is a "black bright spark" who was not fully qualified, but was intelligent, and had power of purpose and determination. He had a dream, but did not know how to achieve it. This could be due to his up bringing or just lack of knowledge.

All I did was offer some guidance, advice, and direction, which helped him, achieve his success. He is now helping other "black bright sparks" to achieve their success because he accepts that he got to where he was because he was mentored and given a helping and guiding hand. No one is self-made. I find it so amusing when the media refer to someone as a "self-made millionaire". That person must have received assistance and advice along the way, plus I am sure they had a team of people running their empire who had given them professional advice to steer their decision.

Mentoring is mutually beneficial; at least, I have always found it that way. I have learnt so much from those that I have mentored, whether younger or older. They have always given me something to think about and to take away from each session. I have always used the 360-degree feedback mechanism with those I mentor. I ask them for feedback on how they feel I am helping them. Inquire what else they would like to see me do to get them closer to their goal or dream. I find this an important tool, as it will help you adjust and focus on what is pivotal to their success.

Mentoring is very rewarding, and it gives one a sense of pride and fulfilment, especially when you see someone you have mentored achieve their goal. It gives you an unexplained inner glow and feeling that you can only experience, if you mentor. So, what are you waiting for? Go.... Go.... Go. Find someone to mentor and experience this for yourself.

Sharing your knowledge and experiences

Mentoring can be time consuming and not everyone has the mental capacity to be a mentor. I get that, but sharing your knowledge and experience is simple and very effective. As a "black bright spark", especially if you are on your way to achieving your goals and dreams, you have an "obligation", to help your fellow black brothers and sisters to realise their dream. I can see your face right now, and hear you thinking: "WHAT! – why should I be obligated to help anyone when they had nothing to do with what I have achieved or where I have reached in my life?" The bold answer is YES; you do have an obligation.

You have an obligation to leave the next generation in a much better state than where you found it. You have an obligation to society and to black people the world over to ensure that they rise back to the level of prominence and dominance that we once had, and deserve. You have an obligation to help mash down those lies, perceptions and stereotypes that permeate about black people in the corporate world and the wider society. Start reaching out to younger "black bright sparks" in your field, your company, and your community, and share your knowledge and experiences. Accentuate the positives, but be truthful, fair and honest in your sharing. Let mentees know there will be challenges, brutal battles and turmoil that they will have to overcome. Don't leave them with misnomers and misconceptions of the journey they are to embark on to achieve their greatness and #CreateAmazing.

Reach out and offer an olive branch to those "black bright sparks" in the company you work in. Seek them out; no matter how far they are. With technology and social media, there are no longer barriers or borders to how we can communicate. Use whatever means you can to get to them and offer that help. This is especially urgent if you find yourself climbing that ladder and getting through those doors. Don't close those doors behind you; leave them ajar so another "black bright spark" can see the gap in the door and know it is open for them to enter. Don't pull up the ladder. Leave it down and leave arrows pointing the way.

There are many ways of reaching out. Join network groups, or start them. When I first started at one the big five consulting firms in the UK, I had a really hard time assimilating and getting my feet on the ground, especially as someone who was coming from industry with little consulting experience. I was one of a handful (and I mean one hand) of black persons in a senior management role especially in my division. Even though I had some guidance, it was not enough to get me started at a level that would allow me to achieve fast enough, being the go-getter "black bright spark" that I am. I realised that others coming in would be faced with the same issues, so with the approval of my divisional head, I started a network called New Hire Support (NHS). The aim was to seek out other newly experienced hires and help them assimilate faster into the organisation, so they could hit the ground running much quicker. We gave them guidance on how to get certain things done in a much shorter time frame. We told them who were the best leaders in the organisation and where to find help and guidance on most things related to their role.

Later in my career, in a senior role in another organisation, I started the Ethnic Minority Mentoring Circle to assist other members of the workforce with advice, guidance and knowledge on performing their roles more efficiently and effectively, achieving the promotion in the organisation they deserved.

I have met other upcoming professionals in one of my areas of expertise; Supply Change and Operations Management, with whom I have shared best practises, tools and templates on how to get things done more efficiently. This was not a mentoring situation, but a pure sharing of knowledge and experience that has helped the mentees to achieve phenomenal results and leave positive memorable experiences.

Become a philanthropist

Philanthropy is not only reserved for the wealthy; although, it will make life much easier, since you can give more without worrying about your own bills. There are numerous ways you can be a philanthropist and give back to your community and the wider world. No matter how small you think it is, as long as it is making an impact on one individual, improving their life and making them better, you are making a difference, and it counts. I strongly believe that one of the most fundamental purposes of each human being is charity; love.

My Gran always used to tell us as children that whatever you give with a willing and pure heart, you would receive a million-fold in return. I have proven this time and time again in my life. I have been truly blessed throughout my life, not only because of my own attitude and gratitude, but also because of my charity towards others. I love giving without looking to receive anything back, and I only give if I truly believe and feel it's the right thing to do.

I never do something just because I want to follow the crowd or to keep up with the Joneses. Sometimes it's not until long after I have done the deed that the recipient or someone else would also say to me how selfless that was or express such gratitude that I realised exactly what I have done.

In 1998, I gave up a lucrative contract and scaled back my business to go and work for one of the largest charities in the Caribbean, Food for the Poor, much to the annoyance of some family members and friends. They could not understand why I would make such a drastic and life-changing move.

At the time I was struggling with the direction I should take my life. I was having drinks with a friend of mine one evening who was the Executive Director of a Catholic Charity in Jamaica, and he said, "You should be grateful for what you have achieved so far, man; if you want to really know about struggle and gratitude, you should work with the poor, then your entire perspective would change". I thought about it for a while and decided there was nothing I had to lose. It was one of the best decisions I made in my life, and it turned out to be the most rewarding two years of my life.

During those two years, I understood clearly why my mother and grandmother would have given their last penny or last morsel of food to persons who had more need. I understood why Mrs. Walker the wife of the rich orchard owner for whom my grandmother sewed, Mrs Hyatt who owned the local shop, Uncle Busha who became my father after the death of my father, my big cousin Sister Paulette (as we called her), and so many others would just give to me and my brothers and sisters, unconditionally, and with such generosity.

It's because of the complete and utter joy that they feel and bring into their lives from being charitable.

During those two years of working with the poorest of the poor throughout the Caribbean, I experienced such peace and joy that my life changed completely. I started being far more appreciative and grateful for what I had in life and started showing more gratitude for the blessings that were unfolding in my life. My Gran always says that when you do good deeds, it will be repaid – even in posterity. I guess I am still living off the blessings of my mother and grandmother. It was not until I worked with the poor that I knew what true charity was and experienced first-hand, the joy, blessing and abundance that the universe can bestow on you from truly and honestly helping others from your heart and soul.

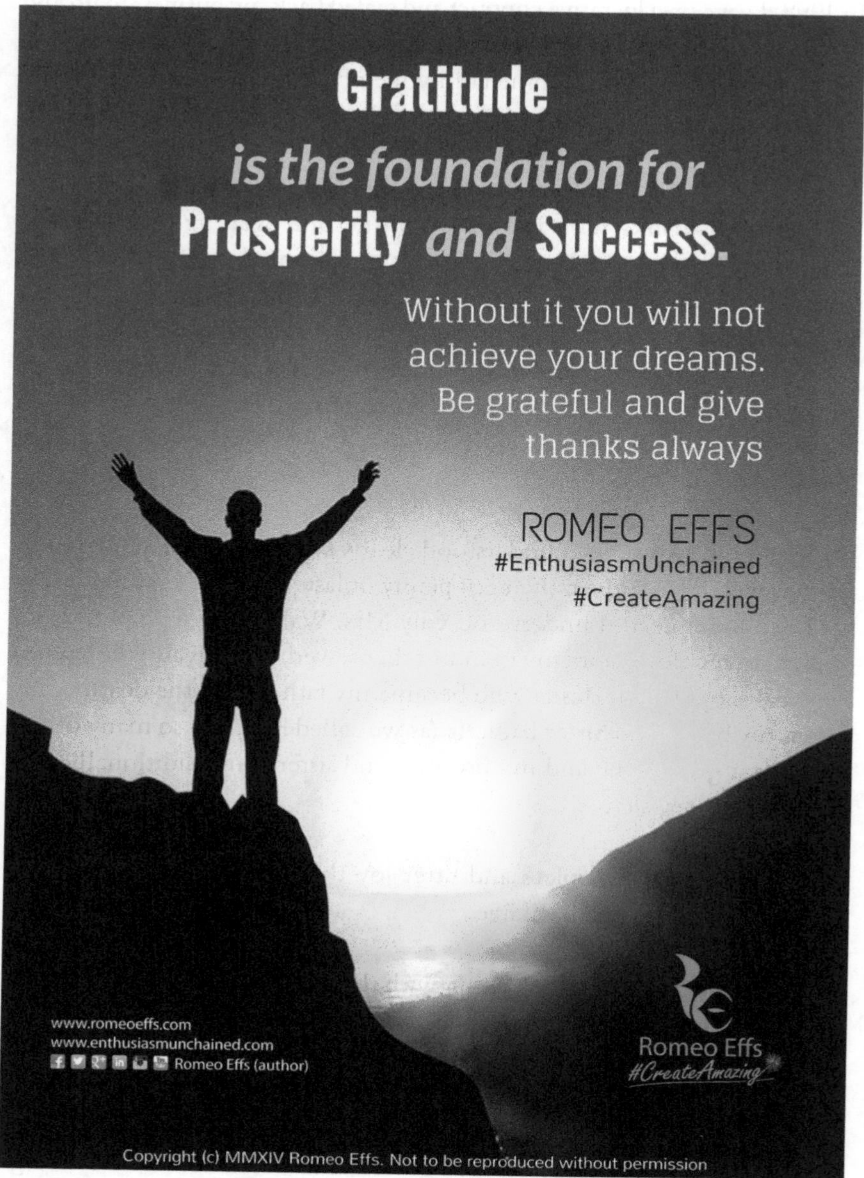

When I left "Food for the Poor", I continued working and helping others, and I made that a central part of everything that I do. People development and prosperity is what I am passionate about. I want to help and see people "#CreateAmazing", deliver phenomenal results, become great, and build empires. That is why I do mentoring and coaching, and have been doing it since I was 25 years old.

That is why I help people in their personal and professional lives to excel, start their own or grow their existing business and make it successful. I have won several awards for one of the UK's largest companies for the work I did in bringing smaller suppliers into their supply chain. Helping people to be empire builders is the reason I have been working with a group of like-minded persons to create a Sports Enterprise Academy aimed at getting more young people from some the most deprived communities to start businesses in the area of sports and sports related industries.

I am not saying that you are to quit your job and go and work for a charity as I did. What I am saying is that being charitable is part of what we are to do on this earth and as part of our life. No matter how small, you will be surprised the significant impact it will have.

A good friend of mine, who is a solicitor, realised that there was an issue with girls in care in Jamaica and other third world countries, and she decided that this was something that tugged at her heart. She did not stand aside and just talk about it, but she organised a small charity and held unique special events to raise funds.

What I found is that we live in a very charitable society and people will give to worthy causes, especially, if you make the event fun. I was part of the project team, made up of some of her friends, for the first fundraising event, which was a huge success. We had a chef blend Jamaican and Italian ingredients to come up with new dishes; we had silent auctions, drinks and a Ska Band playing. There was good food, drinks, music, networking, jokes and lots of fun. Everyone had a great time, and immediately, we had a following for the other events that would follow. This was just one person with a strong feeling to do something from her heart that could affect the lives of others. She laid the first block, and the rest of the blocks fell in place.

Starting your own cause is not difficult, and you can start in your office. I recall sending an email to all the members in my department, asking them to donate new back to school stuff for the Infant school (or Reception

School), I was co-Chairman for a poor community in Jamaica. The email would have a list of the stuff the school would need most.

I would get boxes of pencils, exercise books, crayons, markers, and paper, arithmetic and vocabulary work books, and in some instances, cash donations, which would go towards the provision of a cooked lunch for the students when they attended school. This did not take a lot of effort, just an email and getting the signoff from my department head for a location in the office to store the stuff. There are so many causes that we can get involved in and make a difference. Get involved with something already in existence that truly tugs at your heart. If it does not exist, go ahead with that power of purpose and determination, take that step and "create it… #CreateAmazing.

Volunteering

One of the other things you can do to give back and help to break the stereotype and negative perception is to volunteer. I enjoy giving talks at schools, universities and career fairs. I find youngsters are eager to learn about new and different careers and the different ways that exist for them to become a success.

My career path to date has been wide and varied, spanning numerous roles and industries. I have also started and successfully ran several businesses. I have much to impart to help guide the career paths of those I coach and mentor, and so do you. No matter what your current role, you are way ahead of those youngsters in school or university. They would be more than happy to listen and learn from your experience. No matter how young you are, at what level you are in your organisation, you have something to impart that can make a difference to someone younger and sometimes even older than you.

I find I also learn a lot from these talks as well, as the participants are usually very inquisitive, asking probing questions and challenging your answers, approach and thinking. I really love that and usually leave from there feeling rejuvenated. Plus, it is a lot of fun to watch these youngsters clowning around and just enjoying life before and after the event.

There are numerous organisations that you can sign up to, who will place you in schools around the country or the world to volunteer and give talks or participate in Career Fairs. Better yet, just jump on the phone and call your alma mater and offer to talk to students about a career in what you do or something of interest that you are a subject matter expert in.

I volunteer once a year as a guest lecturer in Supply Chain Sustainability at the business school I completed my masters in, and I also go back to talk to the students of the Logistics Society of which I was President, about careers in Logistics and Transport. I also attend the business school's Careers Fair, and give advice about careers in consulting, supply chain and procurement. All it took was one phone call, and the blocks fell into place.

There are numerous other local community based initiatives that assist the development of the young, the less fortunate, the elderly, etc. that you can also volunteer and get involved in. The only caution I would issue is that you do it because it tugs at your heart. Don't do it, as I said before, because I am writing about it in this book, or because someone else tells you to do it, or you want to follow the crowd. Like everything else in life, if you are not doing it out of pure generosity and love; you will not give your all, and those you are helping will realise this. You will also not receive the abundance of positive favour and blessing that the universe will pour like a flood your way.

Volunteering is especially critical as a "black bright spark", as I have found a severe lack of black role models, particularly males in society. It's not that there aren't a lot of successful black males around, but for reasons known and unknown, they tend to keep their heads buried in the sand, trying to push with all their might and power to get ahead, forgetting that the only way they can be successful is to help to develop others on the way. It's simple; when you are working your hardest, and you find time to help others along the way, the world opens up to you, and you find your journey becomes smoother, and your burden becomes lighter.

Altruism – The key to breaking the negative stereotype mould

Why is it important to break that mould of the stereotypical black person being "angry"? Why is it important to break that mould of the self-perceived "glass ceiling" that is being perpetrated? Why is it important to break that mould that racism is the cause of all our ills, especially in the corporate world? The simple and straightforward answer is because our success as individuals and as a collective group depends on the shattering of these misnomers. That we are greater than the sum of our ambition is worthy of reiteration. It's not one to many that is going to work and break this mould, and demolish those lies. It's one to one, many times. That's the only way! If we each do a selfless act of helping one person along our success journey and teach them the importance of helping and developing others along the way, the impact will be magnanimous… 1-to-1 many times.

I speak to those I mentor and coach about "1 degree of separation". If you get someone to change their mental mind-set, attitude, way of performing, approach, physical appearance or health 0.0001 degree, then over time if they stay on course, you will realise that they have changed course completely for the better, and they will start seeing phenomenal success in their lives.

I am not suggesting that you participate in all of the above-suggested ways of giving back, as it can be time consuming. Believe me, I know! Just find the one or two that you are comfortable doing, that appeals to you and that you will find joy doing and become passionate. Like everything else that I have spoken about in this book, just get started, take that first step and watch the rest of the staircase unfold.

If we want to break that mould, we have to keep sending that message that we can have any dream we want, we can become anything we want to become, and we can be great and #CreateAmazing. To keep a lamp burning, we have to keep putting oil in it. By Mentoring, Knowledge sharing, volunteering, being philanthropic, and altruistic, we can play our small part to chip away at the mould and continue topping up the lamp. As Mother Theresa said, "We ourselves feel that what we are doing is just a drop in the ocean, but the ocean would be less because of that missing drop".

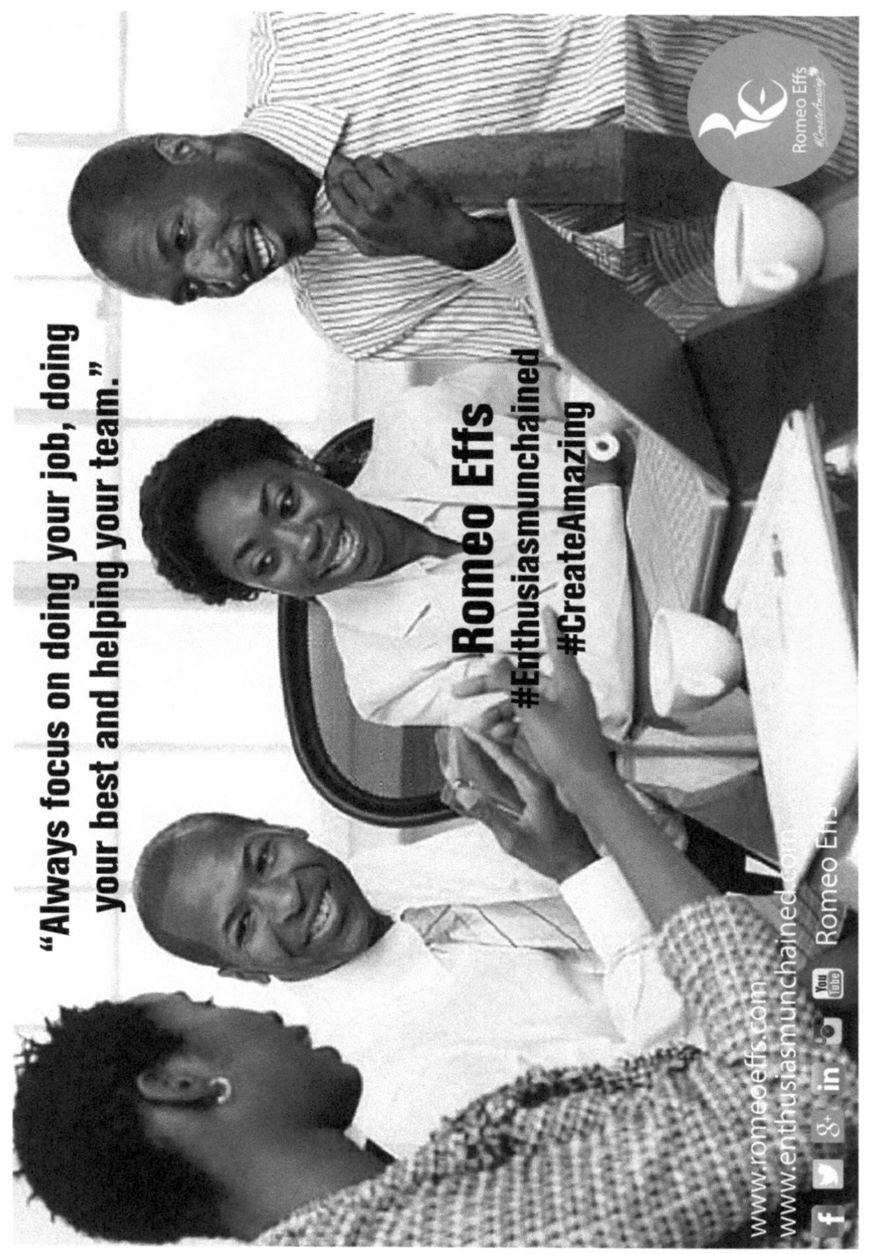
"Always focus on doing your job, doing your best and helping your team."
Romeo Effs
#Enthusiasmunchained
#CreateAmazing
Romeo Effs
www.romeoeffs.com
www.enthusiasmunchained.com
Romeo Effs

Please Listen & Watch
www.enthusiasmunchained.com/EU12

THIRTEEN

My Final Thoughts

"Baby steps count, as long as you are going forward. You add them all up, and one day you look back and you'll be surprised at where you might get to."

Chris Gardner

The power and significance of this quote to my life and this book is that many "black bright sparks" don't know that all they really need to fulfil their greatness is simply to start, no matter how small. They don't realise that it does not take a genius to make things happen, just mere persistence. It reminds me of Christopher Gardener author of *The Pursuit of Happyness*. Gardener who is a world-renowned life coach, author and motivational speaker was raised in a less than ideal circumstance marked with poverty, violence, sexual abuse, family illiteracy and a without a father in his life. Fascinated by finance, but without connections, an MBA or even a college degree, Chris Gardner applied for training programs at brokerages, willing to live on next to nothing while he learned a new trade. Gardner earned a spot in the Dean Witter Reynolds training program but became homeless when he could not make ends meet on his meager trainee salary. Gardner also worked at Bear Stearns & Co from1983-1987 where he became a top earner. In 1987 he founded the brokerage firm Gardner Rich in Chicago from his home with just $10,000. Over the years in addition to expanding its core business as an institutional securities broker, Gardner Rich increased its participation in corporate underwriting and expanded its brokerage services.

Gardener obviously remained focused even though he could have been distracted by many disruptions and family dysfunctions. How he was able to remain focused, alone in the world with little support, his power of purpose and determination, strength and tenacity. Regardless of whatever events he experienced, they motivated him to think, act and do, with a purpose. Today, Chris Gardener's story continues to make history as a "black bright spark".

What I hoped I demonstrated was simply how circumstance and events in one's personal life will play a major role in the story and journey of your life. As long as you have life, you can write your own story of success and #CreateAmazing.

Just keep going!

I leave you with a poem that has inspired me since I was a child.

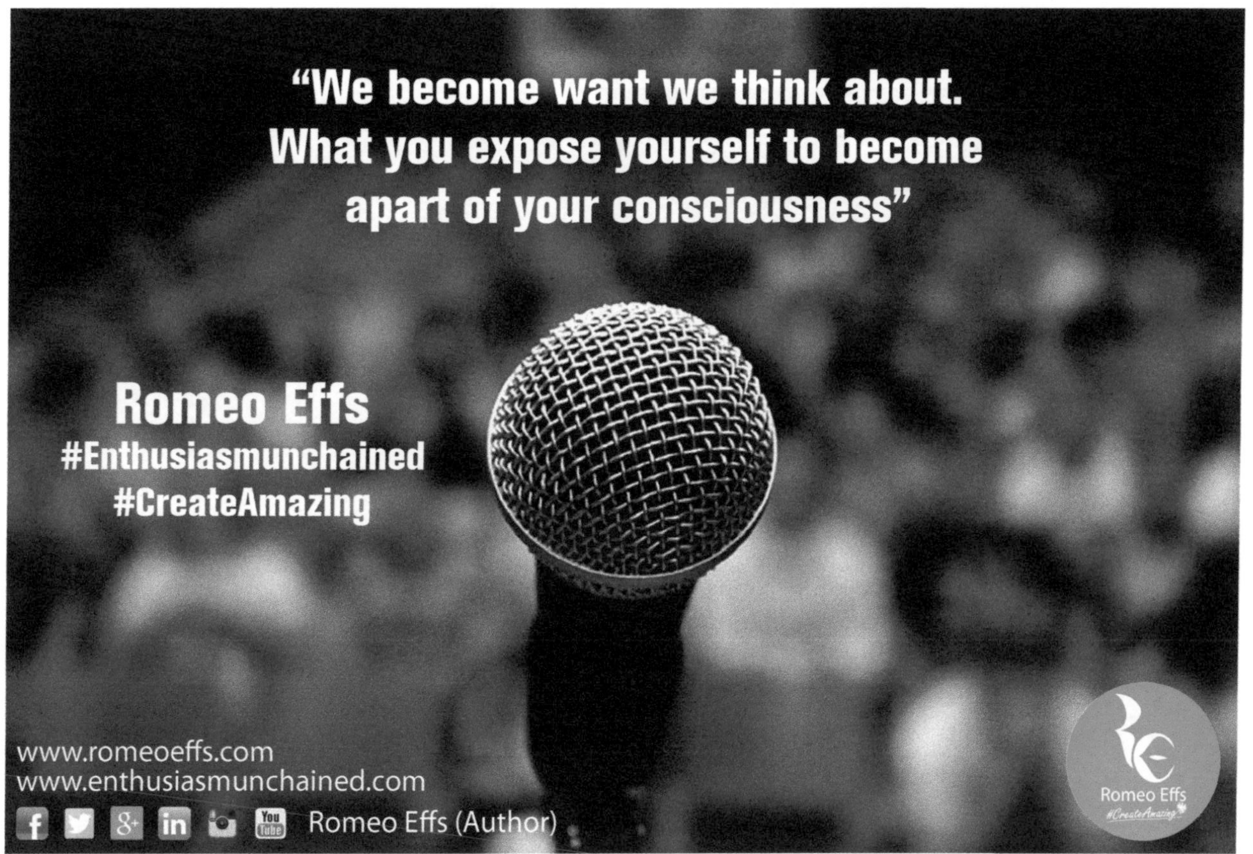
"We become want we think about.
What you expose yourself to become
apart of your consciousness"
Romeo Effs
#Enthusiasmunchained
#CreateAmazing
www.romeoeffs.com
www.enthusiasmunchained.com
Romeo Effs (Author)
Romeo Effs
#CreateAmazing

Please Listen & Watch
www.enthusiasmunchained.com/EU13

Desiderata

by Max Ehrmann

Go placidly amid the noise and haste,
and remember what peace there may be in silence.
As far as possible, without surrender
be on good terms with all persons.
Speak your truth quietly and clearly;
and listen to others,
even the dull and the ignorant;
they too have their story.

Avoid loud and aggressive persons;
they are vexations to the spirit.
If you compare yourself with others,
you may become vain and bitter;
for always there will be greater
and lesser persons than your-self.
Enjoy your achievements as well as your plans.

Keep interested in your own career, however humble;
it is a real possession in the changing fortunes of time.
Exercise caution in your business affairs;
for the world is full of trickery.
But let this not blind you to what virtue there is;
many persons strive for high ideals;
and everywhere life is full of heroism.

Be yourself.
Especially, do not feign affection.
Neither, be cynical about love;
for in the face of all aridity and disenchantment
it is as perennial as the grass.

Take kindly the counsel of the years,
gracefully surrendering the things of youth.
Nurture strength of spirit to shield you in sudden misfortune.
But do not distress yourself with dark imaginings.
Many fears are born of fatigue and loneliness.
Beyond a wholesome discipline,
be gentle with yourself.

You are a child of the universe,
no less than the trees and the stars;
you have a right to be here.
And whether or not it is clear to you,
no doubt the universe is unfolding as it should.

Therefore be at peace with God,
whatever you conceive Him to be,
and whatever your labors and aspirations,
in the noisy confusion of life keep peace with your soul.

With all its sham, drudgery, and broken dreams,
it is still a beautiful world.
Be cheerful.

To your success!
With my love and gratitude

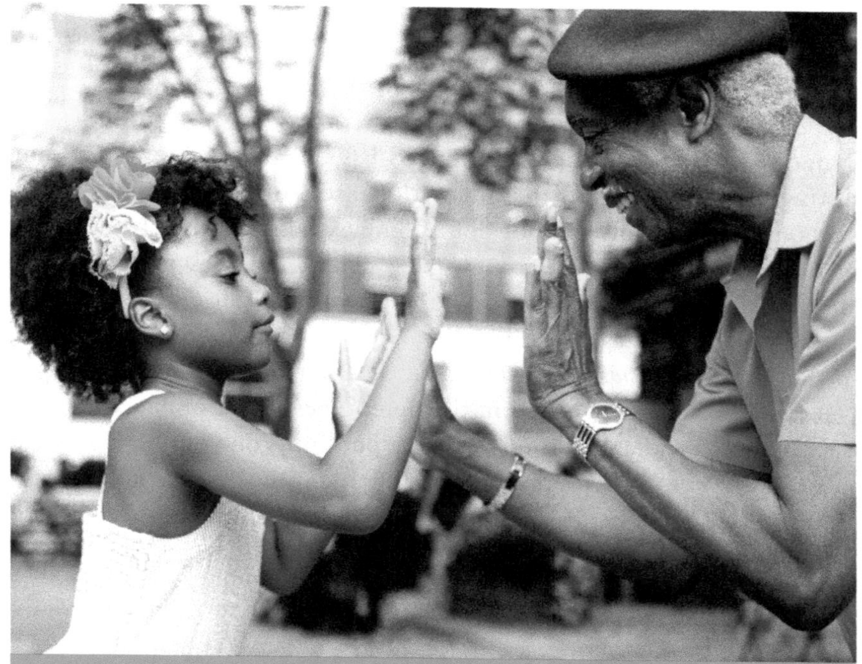

Lebara

Case Study

Lebara: From Guts To Glory

This case study examined how European-based Lebara has positioned and distinguished its brand in the international telecommunications market without the solid nuts and bolts of a complex business plan, bank loans, or external advisors, but through guts, persistence, power of purpose and determination. It explores how the use of the right mind-set, focus, business acumen, integrity, principles, experience and insight, as described in the book *Enthusiasm Unchained*, can help anyone succeed as long as you do not become entangled in the stereotypes, labels of naysayers, the trappings of corporate cultural biases, or put limits on yourself and what you can achieve. The results of the study indicate that it is laser focus, clear purpose, vision and plan of action that are the determining factors for achieving success.

> *Dreams and ambitions are powerful things, and when mixed with power of purpose and determination, and a burning desire, they can be translated into untold successes and riches.*
>
> *Romeo Effs – Author | Entrepreneur | Coach | Speaker*

Background

I conducted the following study on Lebara, a highly successful telecommunications company in London, because the birth of their idea, growth, innovations, monetary success, and charitable mission are a perfect example of how *Enthusiasm Unchained* can energize one's journey into uncharted territories, and propel them through the struggles to achieve stature and phenomenal success.

Yoganathan Ratheeshan was born in Jaffna, Northern Province, Sri Lanka into a modest family with strong morals, values and work ethics. Ratheesh attended boarding school in India until the age of 15 when Sri Lanka's brutal civil war forced his family's move. Upon arrival in the UK, Ratheesh struggled to adjust to the life and especially the language of London. However, he did not give up.

In fact, regardless of what he had to sacrifice, he was determined to succeed. Even though he had to depend on his uncle, to help him with his English work, he eventually completed his secondary studies, went on to university, and majored in Aeronautical Engineering because it was a field dealing with lots of numbers, which he enjoyed.

Ratheesh's persistence to acquire the language, cultural and educational skills that he needed to achieve his goals are examples of his ability to do what it really takes, to get what you really want. After Ratheesh earned his degree as an aeronautical engineer, he decided to pursue a Master's degree, working as a bartender and also selling calling cards to save up enough money for further education. Although he would never return to his Master's degree, I am sure he couldn't have imagined or foreseen the creation of the amazing Lebara story.

Yoganathan Ratheeshan, and his two friends (business partners) Rasiah Ranjith Leon and Baskaran Kandiah, conceived the dream of Lebara. After seeing the architectural masterpiece of the Telenor building in Norway in the early 2000s, the group decided there and then to build a comparable empire. I can only imagine the 'thoughts' that permeated their minds as they agreed to this. This is such a powerful demonstration of a mantra I live by "Thoughts become things".

Problem discovered

While working in the telecommunications industry, and being migrants themselves, the group of friends had realised that there was a problem with charging immigrants high fees to call their native homes. So using their cultural, personal and work experiences, they proposed to deliver a better, low cost product to capture and dominate this special niche in the telecommunications market. Here they realised a specific problem and possible solution. The perfect backbone for any business – identify a problem affecting a large number of people and come up with a solution to solve it.

Solution

Leaning on their strong gut instincts and belief that this would work, Ratheesh, Leon and Baskaran quit their jobs at a calling card company and created the start-up company, Lebara; the name was created from the first two letters of each friend's names, Le-ba-ra. Their mission: to provide affordable and accessible communications for immigrants to stay in touch with friends and family in their home countries. Lebara's Chairman & CEO Ratheesh, who in 2012 won Ernst and Young award for Entrepreneur of the Year, for London and the South, and his partners, were initially refused by many calling card operators. These calling card operators did not realise the opportunity that had arisen as a result of the high charges being levied on a large segment of people living in countries outside of their native homes. In not doing so, they failed to capitalise on a goldmine that was in their hands. They failed to use one of the pillars of success "Anticipation".

Anticipation

Ratheesh and the other co-founders used this pillar of success – Anticipation. They anticipated the needs of the market and saw a problem that needed a solution. Anticipation prepares us to take action so we don't waste time getting ready. Anticipation also helped Ratheesh and his team to create advanced plans to deal with market trends, growth, sustainability, and turbulence. More importantly, it prepared them to stay ahead of the competition. Anticipation, therefore, is a key pillar of success. To overtake the competition or to keep them from encroaching on our niche requires constant vigilance and in-depth anticipation.

Besides anticipating some initial resistance of the calling card operators to provide the credit for the initial inventory, the trio discovered that not everyone grasped or shared their vision. As you go on your success journey, you will also find this, and that's fine. Just remember that the world is full of people with differences of opinions, beliefs, attitudes, and ways of doing things. What's important to remember is that just because someone tells you that you cannot do something or cannot become the person you want to become, doesn't mean they are correct. So go all out to prove that person wrong.

TBO (Think it; Believe it; Own It)

Ratheesh and his partners set out to prove that they were on to something and took whatever actions they needed to bring their vision into reality. However, they did not let "no" be the only or final answer. They had already TBO'd – Thought it possible; Believed it through their vision; Owned it by taking the required actions. Fortunately, after several rejections, they won over ONE operator who agreed to a 55,000 Euro credit line for 14 days. In fact, they actually sold all cards in only three days, pitched their idea once again to operators who had initially rejected them, and then presented that hard cash. Regardless to how many "no's" we hear, we only need ONE "yes". So, keep asking!

Focus

While some might have considered Lebara a high-risk company, Chairman & CEO Ratheesh, believed otherwise. Ratheesh said, "To me, I don't look at both sides of the coin, only the one side; which means that once you have decided to do something, you have a goal, you just run with it". One important factor to note is that Lebara knew its targeted market, and that they could reach, engage, and challenge it with their own concept and unique brand. Knowing your market will help you to successfully target it, and present your unique brand. Everyone in Lebara will tell you that integrity plays a vital part in how the company operates. The CEO Ratheesh, who sets the tone, stated: "It was necessary to establish a clear sense of legality and accountability early on, keep the books straight and maintain a good business ethos – so people don't play around". He was focused on the vision of building a true and ethical empire. This focus set the stage for the heart and consciousness of mind they needed to succeed.

State

This mindset gave them the grounding, as pointed out in my book, to realise that success comes in many packages, shapes, and sizes; there is no one size fits all as far as success is concerned. You need to determine what success looks and feels like to you, and use all this energy to muster and propel yourself there. This is evident in everything Lebara does. The CEO sets the pace, and so Lebara's success is not only measured by the quality of their brand and the engagement with the customer base, but also in achieving their ultimate goal of being the brand of choice for one billion by 2020. Indeed, they are dreaming big, moving fast, and are seemingly unstoppable.

Like Ratheesh and the Lebara team, focus on your purpose and vision for the future and create the right state of mind to write your story so you can take the needed action. Keep your purpose and the vision of what you want to be and to accomplish in the forefront of your mind, your "dangling carrot." Never lose this vision inside your head. You should eat, sleep, walk and talk with this vision being central to your thoughts. All you do should be with this objective in mind. This obsession with your purpose and vision will determine your mindset and your state of being. In the book *Enthusiasm Unchained* I refer to it as "State." Your "State" is your state of consciousness, which includes the feelings, emotions, values and beliefs system that you are prepared to use and act upon to make your vision a reality. Lebara has a "Focus" – which is its clarity of purpose, and a vision of what success means to the organisation. It has the right "State" – the culture and attitude that permeate the organisation with whatever they conceive and believe, they can achieve with their "never give up approach".

Story

As highlighted in my book *Enthusiasm Unchained*, there are numerous inventors and achievers from every walk of life to whom we can look for inspiration. "Others have achieved greatness before you. They are of different ages and from different countries, but their journey and stories are similar. You will have different circumstances to those of your friends and peers. You may be from a much poorer background, have attended different schools, lived in different communities, have different types of parents, and differ in religious beliefs and social values, but the one thing that binds you all is that drive, belief, and power of purpose and determination to succeed" (Effs, 2014). This was central to the Think it, Believe it, and Own it (TBO), mind-set of the of Lebara's founders which gave the company one of the most endearing traits and its "state", which can be characterized as a "never give up" approach. This approach helped them to conceive and "write" the story, the plan, the strategy of how they would achieve their vision, objective-by-objective, goal-by-goal and task-by-task.

Action

Ratheesh and his partners thought of success as abundant, with no limitations, no boundaries, and definitely no glass ceilings; and they dreamt big. Hence, it's no surprise that Lebara's aspirations are to achieve bigger and better things than those whom they admired and those who inspired them. Lebara used this energy to act and propel them in the right direction, and to focus on what they can control. This is indeed what you should strive for in your careers and your business endeavours, take decisive action on the things you can control.

The organisation uses its energy to control, develop, and grow those things that it can influence. "You cannot control what people think or say about you, but with time and by your actions, you can influence it" (Effs, 2014). Lebara is influencing the market place by becoming a high performer and delivering quality service to its customer base, which is one element they have total control over. Examining the company, it's evident that the way in which people perceived them and thought of them changed significantly. It is indisputable that whether in our career or business it's wasted energy to focus on things outside of our control.

Just as Lebara's founders could not control what others believed or thought about them or the competition from the big players, you have to realise and overcome the false or superficial barriers, which hinder or shield us from maintaining a solid focus and achieving your vision. Instead, focus on our purpose and your dream, which in turn drives our state of mind and emotion to build a compelling story, to take inspired action. Hindrances like "racism" are just another mechanism to get "us" off track and keep us "in our place", causing us to be fearful. We become fearful of success, fearful of the organisation, and fearful of taking risks. Fear bolsters that inner critic, who prevents us from taking bold action to be a phenomenal success in our careers and businesses, and prevents us from leaving a legacy in this world.

Guts to Glory

Lebara's aim is to be the "Brand of Choice" for one billion people worldwide by 2020. Although Lebara's founders faced obstacles in 2001 when they tried to turn their vision into reality, they did not allow any negative perceptions of them or their idea, that as businessmen who were not part of London's culture and city business network, they would have a very difficult time finding support and being successful.

Ratheesh has stated, "Contrary to what people say, I think the capital's business scene isn't tied with red tape (barriers). Things are simple here; you don't need to have connections in the government to make it big here." According to Ratheesh, London has been instrumental to his career and success in business and it's the best place to do business. "I don't see any better place than London to succeed in life. If you can't succeed here you can't succeed anywhere," he declared.

To obtain success requires action, and we must understand that while we may speak or write our way into a role, job or task, that only consistently high performance will keep us there and moving to the next levels. The only way we can change our status, position, or circumstances in the corporate world is by achievements. The only way we can build and grow a business is through finding a problem, delivering a solution, and giving exceptional service.

One of the things I always tell my clients as a coach and mentor is "change is measured by achievements not by words and speech". So, just like Lebara's founders, prove people wrong when they tell you that you cannot do or achieve something, or when they say it's impossible to do. There may be those who doubt that Lebara can become the brand of choice for one billion by 2020, but that is not Lebara's focus. Their actions are sharply focused on achieving this goal.

"Prove to the "naysayers" that they are wrong, by becoming great business leaders, achieving phenomenal results, accomplishing things that have never been thought of before, and becoming extraordinarily successful. Make sure that it's seen and felt so that it cannot be denied" (Effs, 2014). Lebara is certainly doing this.

People, like Ratheesh, who become wealthy and successful get there because they think and dream of wealth, abundance, and success. They thought about it, envisioned it, and believed that they could conquer the barriers and obstacles; and then, they moved towards achieving this with the power of purpose and determination; they took action. Ratheesh and his business partners decided their fate and fortune with scribbles on a napkin. Yes, a simple napkin, not a fully fleshed out professional business plan.

Don't become disenchanted or discouraged if you slip on the first step. There is no one who has attained success without failure. Lebara had five attempts trying to break into the Spanish market, however, what's most important is that they kept persisting and succeeded on the sixth try.

Lebara's Chairman & CEO Ratheesh, believes in all heart and consciousness that it's not necessarily what you know, or what you don't know—it's about what you believe in that's important. If you pour your heart into your dreams you can make it happen. It's the focus that indicates your state and your story. With the right "state" of mind, and the courage to act thoughtfully, you will be successful in whatever you do. Focus with a purpose to ensure that your actions achieve the desired results. Embrace change because it's the only thing that is constant. "*We must be the change we want to see in the world". Mahatma Gandhi*

Subject Matter Experts

A subject matter expert (SME) takes advantage of any opportunity to learn the knowledge or skill required to get them to the next level. Being a SME has its advantages. Ratheesh worked in a bar by night, and in a shop selling call-time cards in the day. Ratheesh observed the company's earnings and determined that something was not adding up correctly. Once his boss came down from head office, and Ratheesh told him that the company was losing money on calls because of a miscalculation. A couple of days later the boss rang back with his accountant on the line.

Ratheesh talked him through the problem that he'd discovered. Ratheesh said that his boss was screaming for half an hour, before asking him if he would like to come and work at the head office. In becoming a Subject Matter Expert (SME), Ratheesh went on a training course and learned about the technology needed to produce Lebara's own phone cards. This is a key component that's responsible for helping Lebara to succeed.

Giving Back

Ratheesh and his team, like me, believe strongly that we have an obligation to leave the next generation in a much better state than how we found it. In my book Enthusiasm Unchained I speak about the importance of paying it forward by Giving Back. There are numerous ways we can become philanthropists and give back to our communities and the wider world. No matter how small we think it is, as long as it is making an impact on one individual, improving their life, and making them better, we are making a difference, and that counts. I strongly believe that one of the most fundamental purposes of each human being is charity as referred to as love.

In 2005, Lebara created the Lebara Foundation to help displaced children in disadvantaged areas of the world, many of them homeless, without access to schools, or even a medical clinic. Ratheesh says, "The aim of the Lebara Foundation is to provide sustainable solutions to help displaced children around the world by giving them access to housing, food, clean water and education." The Lebara Foundation is very close to the founders' hearts and a fundamental part of Lebara's values and culture. They are passionate about giving back and making a difference to the communities of their customers.

Mentoring

Mentoring is very rewarding and gives you a sense of pride and fulfilment, especially when you see someone you have mentored achieve their goal. It gives you an unexplained inner glow and feeling that you can only experience if you mentor. Lebara's partners were young (in there twenties) when they embarked on the Lebara journey. They are not just keeping their successes to themselves. In fact, they encourage and support budding entrepreneurs internally, providing the needed mentoring and coaching from their experience to help employees with ideas make their own dreams a reality.

Lebara wants to pay their success forward by championing and supporting talent within their organisation. In doing so, they want to create a culture of change—one that aspires to enable those with the talent and persistence to pursue their own dreams. Lebara is committed to mentoring and has financed a few start-up ventures from Lebara workers. Mentoring can be time consuming and not everyone has the mental capacity to be a mentor. I get that, but sharing our knowledge and experience is simple and very effective.

Your perception of who you are and what you will become is going to be your springboard to #CreateAmazing and greatness. This is far more important than what others perceive of you. It's the lack of this kind of mind-set, I believe, that is the stumbling block to us reaching out more to give a helping hand to our fellow brothers and sisters. We are greater than the sum of our own ambitions, and if we each help one, it will multiply and snowball from one to one, and then to many. Lebara does this by allowing its workers to submit an idea for funding consideration.

Lebara expanded its charitable efforts when it created "The Entrepreneurial Way"; launched at London's Cass Business School (my Alma Mater), to enable young talented student entrepreneurs to appeal for funds to make their business visions a reality. Along with funding, the students would receive additional support and mentoring to help them to navigate the real business world. Students are taught the culture of entrepreneurialism, corporate structure and organisational governance.

Becoming a High Performer

Lebara is a high-performing business. Becoming a high performer is an essential ingredient and pillar for success. Let's consider a few essentials to becoming a High Performer, and why Lebara falls in this category:

1 **Know what performance looks like**: Knowing what performance (success) looks like establishes upfront what is expected of you, what

you are expected to deliver, when you should deliver it, and what will be the outcomes of our tasks. It also sends a clear signal to the organisation that you are prepared to deliver phenomenal results. From the start, the founders of Lebara knew what success would look like for them. They clearly knew in Norway that they wanted to build an empire and how that empire would perform. As they continue on the success journey they revise this expectation and now know what is expected of themselves and their employees, and what their products and services must deliver. Becoming the brand of choice for one billion by 2020 is definitely preparation to deliver phenomenal results.

2 **Exceed expectations**: My little secret, which I will now share with you, is to always under promise and over deliver. I do this for one main reason: experience has shown me over the years that there are always unforeseen circumstances. Things can and will go wrong no matter how well we strategise, plan, and organise in the workplace because we are never in total control. Also, know your limits and, where necessary, partner with experts – just as Lebara understands the importance of working with the right partners to provide the right technological solutions.

3 **Leave memorable experiences**: One of the best ways that I found to leave a memorable experience is to consistently be good at delivering phenomenal results that exceed expectations. Leaving memorable experiences is about the quality of work we deliver. Always ensure quality over quantity. Leaving memorable experiences can be expressed in a number of ways. We could ensure our project delivers something for all stakeholders involved. It could be that we enhance a process by creating a more efficient way of "doing things" for our team and the organisation. It could be that we design and implement a programme that gives the company public recognition, like winning awards for the service we deliver. Lebara has already won several rewards recognising their outstanding successes. Furthermore, Lebara is set to leave memorable experiences through its mentoring programmes, charitable foundation, new initiatives to always deliver its customers value for money, and through its new project, Lebara Community, an online resource providing valuable and compelling information for new and existing migrants, as well as those thinking of migrating.

The Story Continues

The telecommunications industry in Europe will never be the same because Lebara totally revolutionised and transformed it, allowing an under-served segment of the market to do something very important to them – to stay in contact with family and friends in their home countries, and by providing this at exceptional value and super great ease and service. What better memorable experience than that could you ask for? Additionally, Lebara has received several distinguished awards in customer service and has positioned itself in an unorthodox manner as a leader in the telecommunications industry.

This case study is just a snapshot of Lebara's story, a journey that is clearly not complete. Each day, Ratheesh and his team at Lebara are constantly writing new chapters in their success journey to delivering phenomenal results for its stakeholders, making memorable experiences possible for its customers, and leaving a legacy that will last for generations. However, although the phenomenal results of their success cannot be denied, reaching their goal of being the brand of choice for one billion people in 2020 will be a strong testament to their persistence, power of purpose and determination, evolution and legacy.

ACKNOWLEDGEMENTS

The manifestation of this book would not be possible without a number of people and those of you who have contributed in reviewing, researching, or assisting in any other shape or form, especially my team at RSPE Group (now Aspyre Group), to whom I owe a big thank you.

Special thanks to the book project team,

Ousaamah Poyette, from Redi Receipt Books, for project managing the publication process;

Abiodun Oshodi from Geecko Visuals for the book cover design and the designs of all the marketing materials;

Ebenezer Sogunro, for the wonderful job in designing all the illustrations, and for putting up with my demands and request for reworks;

Richard Imonikhe, my Personal Trainer, Administrative Assistant and IT Specialist, for all the research, and all the technical tasks he had to do; Thanks for always being available whenever I hollered, Rich; you are super amazing!

Ainsley Bell, for designing the database to collect the data from the landing page for the book promotion and giveaway;

My dear friend Dawn Lowe; you have an incredible eye for detail, and this book would not have been the same without your input.

Dr. Jenny Remington-Hobbs; my friend, coach, councillor and spiritual guide, thank you for believing in me and my ability to #CreateAmazing. You are a super special person.

I would also like to give a big thank you to my friends, Kwabena Agyie Badu, Ingrid Riley and Dennis Tyson for all the support and understanding they gave me during this process – I will always appreciate all they did;

And I could not get away from thanking my family, especially my children – Damion and Lamour, for understanding when I was not available to help with homework, speak to them, or play with them while I was writing this book. I will make it up to them!

And finally, big heartfelt thanks to all the pioneers who set the pace and stage for me, and who have inspired and motivated people around the world to realise and achieve their greatness; persons such as Martin Luther King, Jr., Anthony Robbins, Nelson Mandela, Les Brown, Oprah Winfrey, Maya Angelou, John Demartini, Marcus Garvey, and Bob Marley, just to name a few. I salute you and hope to continue and improve upon what you have done.

Resources
the Author Recommends

An autographed suit
is created to reflect the
uniqueness of each man
making him an ICON
15%
Discount using
Promotion code
ROM100
AutographedSTYLES
Specially made for today's man
Telephone: +44 (0)3334440173
Address: 145-157 St John Street
London, EC1V 4PW
Website: www.Autographedstyles.co.uk
Email: Soji.O@Autographedstyles.co.uk

THE ACCOUNTING GROUP IS ABOUT MAKING
"PROFITABLE PARTNERSHIP"
Our team love to help and inspire you to grow your business. We will alleviate all your accounting, bookkeeping, taxation and compliance worries and advises you every step of the way.
WE INVEST TIME AND MONEY TO MAINTAIN A TEAM OF DEDICATED AND HIGHLY EXPERIENCED PROFESSIONALS.
Address: Alberminster House
38-40 Sydenham Road
Croydon, Greater London
CR0 2EF, UK
Contact: 0208 680 0086
info@theaccountinggroup.co.uk
www.theaccountinggroup.co.uk
The Accounting Group
Working Smarter Not Harder

SBN
Sterling Business Network
Are you a Business owner or Entrepreneur?
Are you looking for local & international business contacts?
Could you do with more business?
United Kingdom
USA & N. America
The Caribbean
Panama & Americas
Africa & many more

"Amateurs built Google & Apple professionals built the titanic"

You don't have to be an expert to build a successful product. Start from somewhere with expert help from the professionals - us. We make the internet work for you!

GET YOUR BUSINESS STARTED NOW!

Grow your business & reach new heights with our

DIGITAL MEDIA BLUEPRINT

OUR SERVICES

IT CONSULTANCY
MOBILE APP DEVELOPMENT
WEB DESIGN
BRANDING & GRAPHIC DESIGN
SEARCH ENGINE OPTIMISATION
ONLINE MARKETING
SOCIAL MEDIA MANAGEMENT
E-COMMERCE

Rhics Web Studios, a subsidy of Rhics Corporation is a multi-national, full service digital agency and IT Consultancy headquatered in the UK. Specilised in delivering value-added services that facilitate business growth and development in a wide variety of business sectors.

Call +44 333 011 7737
For your free consultation without obligation

info@rhicsstudios.com | www.rhicsstudios.com
facebook.com/RhicsWebStudios @RhicsWebstudios

ABOUT THE AUTHOR

Romeo Effs is co-Founder and CEO of Aspyre Group Ltd., and Founder of Empire Builders Academy.

Empire Builders Academy leverages global experts to provide professionals and entrepreneurs with the vital tools, skills and knowledge, to prepare and inspire them to become successful, personally and professionally whether in the corporate world or as entrepreneurs. It's aim is to see those it works with, dream bigger, reach farther, succeed faster and #CreateAmazing.

Romeo's friends describe him as an overachiever. As a boy he grew up in a poor community in the rural parts of Jamaica. Romeo has been out stripping and baffling his doubters from as early as Primary school where he was teased and bullied because of his weight and mannerism, and where a family member told him that he would end up in the government poor house and amount to nothing. Romeo is a serial entrepreneur and former corporate senior executive. He became a senior executive at the age of 25 and started his first business at age 16. He has worked at a Senior Executive level through out the world in multi-national Fortune 500 and FTSE companies in a variety of industries.

He has also owned and operated in excess of 14 business involved in transport, Film and Entertainment, manufacturing, hospitality, technology, leisure, food, consulting, agriculture and education. He has worked with some of the world's leading global companies all over the world helping them to achieve phenomenal transformations.

His varied experience and knowledge gives me a unique advantage to know what it takes and is needed to grow professionally and in business and the mind-set that is right for success. Through *Empire Builders Academy*, he educates, mentors and coach hundreds of professionals and business owners to take their career, business and their personal life to the next level. Although Romeo works with entrepreneurs and professionals from all backgrounds he has a particular affinity to work with Black, Asian and Minority Ethnic (BAME) professionals and entrepreneurs.

Romeo has been doing coaching and mentoring from as far back as he can remember and have been doing it professionally for the past 10 years. Two of the areas of specialization for him are helping professionals maneuver the corporate environment to gain promotion and success and getting businesses investor ready.

> *"I'm on a mission to educate, inspire and equip people of colour to unshackle their past, embrace the present and look to the future with a mind set of empowerment, abundance & prosperity. The result I want to see in those that I work with, is to see them dream bigger, reach farther, succeed faster. Not only in their profession or business but in their personally life, and for them to have the time to do and achieve the things they love".*
>
> *ROMEO EFFS – ENTREPRENEUR |AUTHOR | COACH | SPEAKER*

Throughout his career Romeo has always pioneered new and innovative ways to drive efficiency and solve complex business challenges. He is a master facilitator and leader who inspires those he works with to deliver phenomenal results, and to be the "best version of themselves".

Romeo is passionate about the development and success of professionals and entrepreneurs and gave up a lucrative corporate career to pursue this dream and passion – teaching and coaching. He has undergone ridicule and indignation from many for this passion and what he feels he is born to do. He has been told it will not succeed; yet he perseveres.

To find out more about Romeo Effs and his remarkable story and get more free training and insight to help you on your success journey, visit Romeo online:

www.romeoeffs.com
www.empirebuildersacademy.com
Romeo Effs (Author)
@romeoeffs
@romeoeffs

Other Products & Services from Romeo Effs

Unshackling Your Success

BOOT CAMP

DISCOVERY SESSIONS

Meet Romeo Online and Receive Free Training at:

Romeo Effs (Author)

@romeoeffs

@romeoeffs

Lightning Source UK Ltd.
Milton Keynes UK
UKHW02f1415141117
312687UK00002B/3/P

9 780993 292804